POWERFUL

Nirupama Subramanian has written a gem of a book. Her fascinating analysis of the six feminine powers is bound to inspire readers and open their eyes to their own deep and unique strengths—strengths with which they can break age-old boundaries.

– Chitra Banerjee Divakaruni, author of *The Forest of Enchantments* and *The Last Queen*

Finally, a book that uses women and power in the same breath, without irony or embarrassment. Using the Indian ethos, the author builds new, empowering archetypes that we can all model ourselves on and be our best own icons.

– Kaveree Bamzai, journalist and author

Self-belief is the key that liberates us from doubts and diffidence to unleash our true potential. Nirupama Subramanian provides guidance on how to do this.

– Kiran Mazumdar-Shaw, Executive Chairperson, Biocon

Nirupama has spent the last few years coaching and training women across India, and has a thorough understanding of the challenges and issues they face. I am thrilled that she is putting all that experience to good use in this new book. The six feminine-power models will help Indian women understand themselves and the world around them better, overcome their limiting beliefs and live their full potential to create a just and equitable society.

– Debjani Ghosh, President, NASSCOM

The biggest question for women leaders remains: how to move forward when there is no playbook for aspiring women in the modern workplace and the path is still defined by men? Indian society is built around a strong gender stereotyping and motherhood model, creating guilt for those who try to move away from it. Women tend to live in self-doubt about deserving their success, and remain fearful of displaying power, since appearing too powerful threatens to lower their likeability quotient—a dilemma men never face. Women, own your success: celebrate small victories, believe in yourself and mentor young women in their journey. You can be powerful and warm at the same time! Nirupama's comprehensive book will further shatter the glass ceiling and challenge gender stereotypes, helping you tap into your inner power.

– Shital Kakkar Mehra, Executive Presence Coach for CEOs; bestselling author; Co-founder, Katalyst (NGO)

More than 40 per cent of my management team consisted of women, both in Nokia and PepsiCo. I learnt a lot from them. Women have more power than they know or use. Their soft power, loyalty to teams and organizations, and the ability to reconsider their point of view when given fresh evidence, give them a unique advantage. Identifying the six feminine types is a great way to help women leverage their power.

– Shiv Shivakumar, Group Executive President, Strategy, Aditya Birla Group

NIRUPAMA SUBRAMANIAN

POWERFUL

THE INDIAN WOMAN'S GUIDE TO UNLOCKING HER FULL POTENTIAL

HarperCollins *Publishers* India

First published India by
HarperCollins *Publishers* in 2021
An imprint of HarperCollins Publishers
HarperCollins *Publishers* India, Cyber City, Building 10-A, Gurugram, Haryana-122002, India
www.harpercollins.co.in

2 4 6 8 10 9 7 5 3 1

P-ISBN: 9789354227028
E-ISBN: 9789354225574

Typeset in 11/14 Joanna MT at
Manipal Technologies Limited, Manipal
Printed and bound at
Manipal Technologies Limited, Manipal

*

HarperCollins *Publishers*, Macken House, 39/40 Mayor Street Upper, Dublin 1, D01 C9W8, Ireland

For Kaavya
You are already powerful.

Contents

1
My Story of Power

'One day, Vasuki was drawing water from the well. Just as she was pulling up the bucket, she heard her husband call her from the house. Vasuki immediately left the bucket and ran to listen to her husband and fulfil his need. When she returned, the bucket was still in the air, hanging just as she had left it.'

I listened rapt as my grandmother narrated this story. We had a well in the backyard of our house in Chennai and I would often watch our maid haul the rusty iron bucket of water up, her hands working hard on the coir rope to ensure the bucket did not drop. It seemed impossible that a bucket would stay suspended in mid-air, defying all the laws of gravity and nature.

But such is the power of a virtuous, obedient woman.

Somehow this story of Vasuki, the wife of the great Tamil poet Tiruvalluvar, has stayed with me through the years. Vasuki was the epitome of the ideal wife. She was so chaste that she turned a handful of sand into warm rice and served her husband a sumptuous meal. She was so obedient that she did not question her husband when he asked her to fetch a lamp in broad daylight. She was rewarded for her devotion and goodness by dying a married woman, a 'sumangali', saved from the terrible fate of a widow. Why did she not use her amazing transformative powers for any other cause? Did she get these powers only because of her devotion to a man?

I did not get any answers to these questions.

When I was about seven-years old, my parents took me to watch a dance–drama based on the story of Savitri and Satyavan. Savitri was a talented and beautiful princess who gave up her wealth and status to marry Satyavan, the impoverished son of a deposed king in exile. Despite being dissuaded by her elders and despite being warned that Satyavan would die within a year of marriage, Savitri insisted on marrying him.

For a year after marriage, she served her husband and in-laws with selfless devotion. Then the inevitable happened. Satyavan died. Yama, the god of death, himself came to take Satyavan away. But the devoted wife refused to give up. She followed Yama doggedly till he was moved by her sincerity and perseverance to grant three boons. Savitri cleverly asked him to bless her with children. The exhausted and absent-minded Yama agreed, not realizing that she needed a living husband to give her the children. I still recall the triumphant face of the voluptuous actress in the shiny green sari as she fell at the feet of her resurrected husband.

What do I remember this story for? Not for Savitri's resourcefulness or resoluteness. I remember it for her selfless love and fidelity to her husband. Why? Because this is what we celebrate. 'Sati-Savitri' is the phrase we attach to this woman, a connotation that implies a woman can only wield her power in the service of a man. Millions of Indian women still fast and perform prayers for the long life of their husbands on a day that is dedicated to Savitri in the Hindu calendar.

Why do we not see Savitri as a powerful woman who used her wit and perseverance to bring a human being back to life?

As I write this, I wonder about the power of the stories of Vasuki, Savitri and others. Stories where women did not make a fuss, did not cross lines, did not question authority and were rewarded. There are other stories too, where they broke rules and were punished. There are stories where they were courageous, resilient and wise. Yet we never recognize them as powerful in their own right. Like Vasuki and Savitri, women through the ages seem to have derived their power from their connection to men and have used it to serve men and/or the children in their lives.

Powerful goddesses—Durga, Kali and Shakti—are divine energies that saved mankind from evil, Lakshmi can bring prosperity into your life or take it all away at her pleasure; but your average woman is not allowed to be a goddess. There is something fearful and even dangerous about a woman in her full power. To survive, we have had to deny our power, the Shakti energy in us. There have been times when I have felt powerless.

I am a 'good girl' from a privileged family. I was an intelligent, hard-working, confident student and felt comfortable enough to use public transport in Class XII. Yet, when a rough male hand groped my body in a crowded bus, I froze. My mouth dried up and I felt a nauseous sensation, that I later recognized as shame. It did not last more than a few seconds and by the time I decided to do something, the man had merrily moved on. After that incident, I made sure that I never boarded a very crowded bus ever again, preferring to wait or walk a distance to await a 'ladies' special' bus that ferried only females.

During meetings at work, senior clients would speak to my male colleague rather than make eye contact with me. Even if I made a statement, the next question would be directed to my colleague. I would get annoyed but never brought up the issue with anyone. It left me feeling just a little less confident as a leader. I dismissed these clients as male chauvinists, but wondered if I had somehow diminished myself. Did I not appear to be someone capable of holding a position of power?

The turning point came when my eight-month-old daughter fell ill with a severe E. coli infection and had to be hospitalized. With her nanny also hospitalized for an emergency surgery, it was a harrowing time for me, as I dashed and darted between the two hospitals, my office and my home, trying to hold everything together. I felt both helpless and angry. Guilt and shame drained my energy at home and at work. I quit my job and vowed never to be in such a situation again. A part of my identity as a supermom, who expertly juggled work and motherhood, had just collapsed. I felt like a failure.

Recently, I travelled to Bengaluru on work. I always make sure that I land before 9 p.m., but my flight took-off late. By the time I got out of the airport and into a cab, it was 11 p.m. I was tense throughout the ride to the hotel and more so when the driver took a desolate road. I stayed glued to Google maps verifying the route throughout the journey, and was immensely relieved when we arrived at the hotel by midnight. I shouldn't have to feel this way, I thought.

I felt powerless because of my gender. But this incident drove another point home: the occasions when I have felt powerless, the powerlessness has almost always been rooted in my gender. The workplace also reflects this power–gender imbalance. In more than two decades in the field of leadership development, I hardly saw any women in senior roles in the companies I worked with. The number of women, in fact, dwindled as seniority levels rose.

In 2018, I set up my own firm GLOW, Growing Leadership of Women, along with my business partner, Aparna. As I started working with women as a coach and facilitator, I noticed how strong those old messages were.

Women face challenges that are a little different from those faced by men. We *do* believe we are in a brave new world and that the glass ceiling can be broken. We *do* want to integrate with the rest of the world and embrace 'modern' values without letting go of our traditions. Women *are* heading companies and thriving as doctors, lawyers, performing artists and entrepreneurs, yet we struggle with questions that mostly never trouble men.

- Should I fast on Karva Chauth for my husband even if I don't believe in it?
- Can I disagree with my bosses when I have been brought up to obey my elders?
- Will I be a bad mother if I leave my child in a crèche and go to work?
- My husband is an abusive alcoholic. My mother tells me that the husband is on a par with god; so he is my 'pati parmeshwar'. Should I leave him, or keep trying to make it work?

As I spoke and engaged with more women socially and at work, I noticed patterns in their actions, language and stories. I realized that there were certain stereotypes that were perpetuated by the world outside, such as the ideal mother or 'adarsh ma' and the good girl with right values or 'sanskari ladki'. I saw certain energies that resided in the women, either flowering fully or struggling to emerge. I saw certain shifts in the way women were portrayed in contemporary films and books, and also the strong grip our age-old stories have on the collective consciousness of women.

This led me to become more interested in the power of archetypes and stories as a source of energy. I realized that progress and feminism for me were not just about claiming positional power, or of putting men in their place. I was excited because I realized there was a possibility for wholeness, for living an authentic life. I don't claim to have reached there. I am still a work in progress, but I know I am on the journey. This book is a part of that journey. I am keen to share what I know with other women in the hope that they may find some ways to embrace their whole selves.

I am not a psychotherapist or a Jungian psychologist, though I have used the principles of psychology extensively in my work. I am a storyteller, a facilitator and a coach. I use the model of archetypes to understand our myths and use this connection to create some 'Aha!' moments for the reader, moments that can move a person from awareness to action. This is not a prescriptive book. I do not believe that the same solutions and tips will work for everyone. It is a means for greater self-awareness and understanding, and provides a path for accessing true power.

The best way to read this book is to first read about a woman's six sources of power. This will help the reader to identify her own power profile and power blocks. You can take the Powerfulife Assessment which is a validated tool and find out your Power Profile. This is available at www.powerfulife.in. Chapter 11, 'Practices to Invoke Your Power', lists concrete actions that anyone can take to invoke a particular power, overcome a power block, and shift from awareness to action. I believe that if we introspect and use the wisdom from the archetypes and stories, we can lead a better life where we are in our full power. I have used this wisdom in my life and continue to use it daily. It has benefitted me immensely whenever I have been able to overcome my power blocks by integrating these powers. The journey is still on but now I have a powerful map. I don't feel lost. I know I will find my way out. I believe that by reading this book, women will better understand their positive qualities and potential derailers. This book is a guide to navigate the unexplored territories of feminine selfhood.

2
Women and Power

What is the first image that comes to mind when you hear the word 'powerful'?

Close your eyes for a few seconds. Who do you see?

For me, it is an image of He-Man. As a child growing up in the eighties, the cartoon show *He Man and the Masters of the Universe* was one my favourites. Young Prince Adam of Eternia held his trusty sword aloft and cried 'By the power of Greyskull!', and was immediately transformed into the tall, hunky, heavily-muscled He-Man, who declared 'I have the power!'

Power was a big, blond man with a long sword.

And so it continues to be.

Power is also a word delivered like a bullet, a sharp slap, a booming explosion and a sleek sword capable of causing immense damage. But it is not a word associated with women. Through most of human history, women have not held positions of power—neither in the household, nor in the external world. On the contrary, women have been systematically silenced, turned to stone, burnt at the stake and erased from history books. The qualities that enable women to nurture, bring life into the world, hold families together and build communities have been deemed weak and irrelevant in a masculine world.

The world today is not in balance. Most corporations and countries are run by men. Power is lopsided. There is an absence of the feminine principle. In fact, any attempt at claiming power is met with a backlash and more repression. On the one hand, we have movements like Me Too where women are speaking up and speaking out. On the other hand, there is increased violence against women—rape, sexual assault, verbal and physical abuse—that doesn't show any sign of going away. Even the United Nations presents a dismal picture of gender equality, pushing back its estimate by a few years every successive year.

As per recent research by the World Economic Forum (Salyer and Cann, 2019), total gender parity at the workplace will be achieved only after 257 years, in 2276! As of now, 188 out of 200 countries are led by men (O'Neill 2021). Almost 80 per cent of seats in parliaments across the world are occupied by men; and 483 of the world's Fortune 500 companies are led by men (Hinchliffe, 2020).

The story is a little different in India, in that the numbers remain dismal even if we look at just the previous two decades. The third National Family Health Survey (NFHS) carried out in 2006 found that 35 per cent of Indian women had experienced physical and sexual violence, and 37 per cent had experienced domestic violence; only 1 per cent of married women had initiated violence against their husbands. In an article written in 2013, 'India: Where a women is killed every hour for dowry', the website *IndiaSpend* quoted data from the Lok Sabha—'63,171 women have been killed in dowry-related incidents from 2005 till 2012, which roughly translates into 7,896 deaths per year, 658 per month and 22 per day. Almost 1 woman died every hour in India due to dowry-related violence.' The NFHS-5 carried out in 2019 showed some reduction in the crimes against women in certain states but crimes against women in the age group 18–49 in Bihar and Kerala was at 40 per cent.

According to latest World Bank (2021) estimates, labour force participation of women in India has declined to 20.3 per cent in 2020 from 29.2 per cent in 2007.

It wasn't always like this.

Once upon a time, long, long ago, I believe that women in India were free, respected and powerful. The worship of the mother goddess and the fertility principle was common in the Indus Valley civilization. The *Devi Suktam*, written by a female sage called Vak who identifies herself with the mother goddess, is part of the *Rig Veda* (c. 1100 BCE) and speaks about the glory of the feminine energy, 'I only breathe forth like the wind, while holding together all living creatures/So great (vast) have I become, possessing greatness, that I am beyond heaven and this earth.'

Women were once equal partners with men. We know of the great and learned ancient sages Gargi and Maitreyi, both of whom were women who held their own against others. Households were led by women who made choices about their lives and also chose the men in their lives. The *Atharva Veda* (c. 1200 BCE) states in one verse, 'O woman, you are the keeper of knowledge of all types of actions' (7.47). Elsewhere it states, 'O groom, the bride is the protector of the entire family. May she dwell in your home for a period and sow seeds of intellect' (1.14.3).

The importance of women's contribution to the family was acknowledged and women were encouraged to study before choosing an eligible husband. No Vedic ritual was complete without the presence of the wife.

There is no definite historical evidence for the origin of patriarchy or the diminishing importance of the feminine principle. In his book *Sapiens* (2014), a vast sweeping account of humanity, author Yuval Noah Harari seems mystified by the universal preference for men over women, 'even though the precise definition of "man" and "woman" varies between cultures, there is some universal biological reason why almost all cultures valued manhood over womanhood. We do not know what this reason is. There are plenty of theories, none of them convincing.'

In the Indian subcontinent, the cult of the mother goddess and worship of the divine feminine was gradually absorbed into the mainstream veneration of the male deities, Shiva and Vishnu. Goddesses began to be worshipped as divine consorts rather than powerful gods in their own right. Myths and stories reflect this paradigm, relegating women to supporting roles, reflecting the mores and morals of that era. Patriarchy had become the new norm. The male was the ultimate symbol of power.

As I read more about power and its implications for women, I realized there are certain differences in the way Western myths treat women and their quest for power, and the way Indian culture deals with them. The backlash against women's claims for power in Western myths is often direct and immediate. In Greek mythology, women are raped often and brutally by the gods. A young Medusa is raped by Poseidon in a temple, and Athena, the goddess to whom the temple is dedicated, punishes Medusa further by turning her hair into a mass of writhing snakes. Poseidon escapes to commit the same crime again, while poor Medusa, transformed into a terrible creature, is forced to live in a cave till she is redeemed by death at the hands of Perseus. Persephone is kidnapped by Hades, raped, forcibly made his wife and then forced to spend six months of each year in his kingdom—the underworld. Philomela is raped by Tereus and then has her tongue chopped-off by him, so that she cannot denounce him as her rapist. History shows that Joan of Arc was burnt at the stake; so were countless others at the Salem witch trials and the infamous witch hangings in the UK.

In the East, especially in the Indian subcontinent, the subjugation and repression of women has been more subtle, more insidious. Practices to keep women from power have become cultural norms stemming from deep-rooted beliefs and women have been co-opted successfully into their own repression. Our myths and stories are also full of cautionary tales, stories of crime and punishment, of rewards and redemption for virtuous women. These have successfully been coded into our DNA and have become a part of our cultural blueprint, to the extent that these norms seem almost 'normal'.

Four main strategies are used by the powerful to retain power and prevent the others—the underclass—from even staking a claim. These strategies have been used intensively and extensively by the system of patriarchy in our culture. Regardless of religion, caste and geography, all women in the subcontinent have been subjected to these strategies to keep them helpless, dependent and unable to realize their own potential.

1. Diminish

The *Manusmriti* (c. 200 BCE), written much later than the Vedas, reflects the strong presence of patriarchy in this period: 'Men must make their women dependent day and night, and keep under their own control those who are attached to sensory objects. Her father guards her in childhood, her husband guards her in youth and her sons guard her in old age. A woman is not fit for independence' (9.2).

A little over two millennia later, while learning Hindi grammar at school, I came across a word used as a synonym for 'woman'. That word was 'abla'. It took me a few years to understand that the literal meaning was derived when it was broken into 'a-bla', i.e., weak or one without strength (bal). Woman = weak.

Portraying women as frail and helpless diminishes them and takes away their power. It diminishes their self-value and erodes their self-worth. Over the centuries, most women have been co-opted into patriarchy and unknowingly collude with it to perpetuate its customs and norms in the name of tradition and culture. The message is so clear and so powerful that it has stood the test of time, and radiated from the scriptures to shine on through popular media, such as advertising and cinema, as well.

Over time, women have bought into this notion of male superiority and the dominance of the husband in a marriage; and every mother perpetuates the same with her daughter. Since the husband alone is considered a wife's refuge, many parents refuse to offer shelter or succour to a married daughter ill-treated by her husband. Thus, the message is passed down from mother to daughter, reinforced by the mother-in-law, and ratified by scriptures and even society. Sati and jauhar (two practices of widow burning), child marriage, taking the veil or 'purdah', female infanticide, dowry—are all customs perpetuated by men but also by women themselves.

Women have bought into the notion that the weak woman needs protection because she is not strong enough to defend herself. In fact, one of the reasons why domestic abuse is not reported or spoken of in India is the complicity of the woman in the notion that she somehow deserves it, or that she cannot do anything about it. Mary, my house-help, often spoke of her deceased husband, a drunk who would thrash her for not giving him money to buy alcohol or on some other pretext. 'What could I do? He was a man,' was her explanation, when I asked why she hadn't left him. Mary herself was powerless to stop her son from beating up his wife Valli, a poor voiceless creature who eventually succumbed to her injuries.

The heroines of our great epics, the Ramayan and the Mahabharat never entered into the battlefield or fought for themselves. Sita waited for her husband to rescue her, so that he could uphold his 'maryada' (which may be loosely translated as prestige or honour linked to the carrying out of one's duty). Draupadi needed the Pandavas to avenge her humiliation. Princess Amba had to be reborn as a man, Shikhandi, to take revenge on Bhishma.

The role of the damsel in distress, waiting for a man to rescue or avenge her, has been so deeply entrenched in our psyche that most of our movies depict the hero as the saviour. It is unseemly for a woman to raise her voice and fight her own battles.

This narrative is perpetuated by well-meaning parents and relatives who keep young girls sequestered and sheltered from the real world. I remember an incident from the Holi celebrations in our condominium in Gurugram. Two little girls came up to me and complained, 'Aunty, the boys are troubling us.' I could see three little boys lurking in wait, their plastic 'pichkaris' filled with coloured water to squirt at unwary victims. Without a second thought I began marching up to them, ready to scold; but midway I realized the message I was sending the girls: that they could not defend themselves and needed an adult to stand up to boys their own age. I returned and told the girls to tell the boys off. They needed to get their own pichkaris.

They hesitated.

'Don't worry,' I assured them. 'I am here. If they misbehave, I'll come over. Be brave.' And I watched apprehensively as they went up to the boys. I heard loud voices. One of the girls got squirted with water. The other wrenched a pichkari from one of the boys and ran away. They were playing Holi and it was fine. I felt rather proud of myself. I hope the girls learnt something useful. I learnt that it was almost a 'natural' or perhaps a 'culturally programmed' protective instinct to keep girls safe.

However, this desire for the safety and protection of girls is what continues to propagate their belief in their own vulnerability and has kept them scared and secluded.

2. Decorate

The Ayodhya Kand in the Valmiki Ramayan states, 'Through service to one's husband, even that woman who does not offer salutations to anyone other than her husband and is averse to the worship of gods secures the highest heaven.' In the Tulsidas Ramayan, Anusuya, the noble wife of Rishi Atri, tells Sita, 'A woman is impure by her very birth; but she attains a happy state by serving her lord (husband).' Servitude and submission to a man, especially the husband, has been elevated to a noble virtue and it is this virtue alone that can elevate the impure-by-her-very-birth woman.

If a woman toes the line by sticking to the roles assigned to her by the mores of society—as a 'good' daughter, a 'good' mother, and most important of all, a 'good' wife—she is considered worthy of praise and is 'elevated' in status by the showering of not just praise and affection, but also by being decorated with jewels, costly raiment and other gifts. For all her chastity and obedience, the woman does not gain anything tangible by right—no independence, no respect, nor anything else substantial in the present life—in return for all that she does; unless it is *given to her* by another's choice.

Thus if she produces sons and keeps her husband and in-laws happy, she may (but there's no guarantee) be given jewels, praised, and even be deified. If not, she has to believe that virtue is its own reward. The Hindu concept of 'pati parmeshwar' (the husband as god) threatens the wife straying from the path of chastity and obedience, with the wrath of god. However, if she stays on the path, respectfully bowing to the wishes of her lord and master, she will be rewarded with respect and affection, if not in this life then surely in the next one.

Even the blessings traditionally given to Hindu women are different from those given to men.

- *Sada suhagan raho* (May you always be a wife; implying, never a widow)

- *Dheerga sumangali bhava* (May you long remain a wife; implying, the sumangali is the virtuous one, whose merits bestow her husband a life longer than her own.)
- *Sau putravati bhava* (May you be the mother of a hundred sons; obvious implication regarding daughters!)

The men are told something else.

- *Ayushman bhava* (May you live long)
- *Vijayi bhava* (May you be victorious)

There is no mention of wife or children.

A woman's ultimate reward in such a milieu is earned at death, provided she predeceases her husband. This much-prized wish—to predecease the husband—usually stems from a wish to escape the pathetic life that widows often lead in their later years. Sati (practiced fairly commonly until a couple of centuries ago in parts of India) was a socially sanctioned escape from the deprivation and powerlessness of a widow's life. However, the truth is that the women most likely were (and in stray cases still are) coerced by the family (read in-laws) to 'volunteer' for sati.

As recently as 1987, eighteen-year-old Roop Kanwar from Rajasthan supposedly overcome with grief, jumped into the funeral pyre of her husband and died. Many eyewitnesses said otherwise. While there were arrests and charges of attempted murder after this event, eventually all the accused got off scot-free. Many people lauded her act which supposedly upheld our traditions (Rajalakshmi, 2004). There is now a small shrine dedicated to her in the village of Deorala, where she lived.

Thirty years later, everyone agrees that sati is not relevant, while continuing to show respect for Roop Kanwar's choices.

India also boasts a large and ornate Rani Sati Temple in Jhujhunu in Rajasthan, which is visited by thousands of devotees and is dedicated to a woman who immolated herself after her husband's death (said to have taken place sometime between the thirteenth and seventeenth centuries). Devotees address her as Rani Sati Dadiji (or Rani Sati, our paternal grandmother).

While alive, women have to live up to impossibly high standards. We live with the fear that we may never be good enough, worthy enough or even just enough. All the striving for a Good Conduct Prize leaves us too drained to attempt or achieve anything else. Vague promises and dubious rewards have served to keep us in a constant state of anxiety.

3. Deter

The third strategy is to deter women from indulging in any behaviour that could lead them to claim their own identity or power. This is similar to the way animals are trained to obey and fall in line—a treat for a trick; a whipping to tame any wildness. No Indian woman is immune to the various 'Lakshman rekhas' or boundaries drawn ostensibly for their own protection by family and society. Crossing the boundary will bring shame, ruin and disaster for the woman and her family. She needs to stay within the four walls of her house 'for her own good'.

Any woman who transgresses cultural norms is punished. Even poor Shakuntala of Kalidasa's immortal classic *Abhigyana Shakuntalam*, whose only sin was to be distracted and negligent towards a guest, was cursed and abandoned by her husband.

Ahalya, who was tricked and seduced by the ruler of heaven Indra, was turned to stone. Ravan's sister Shoorpanakha dared to express her desire for a man and had her nose cut-off. Today, thousands of years later, a woman who chooses to exercise her freedom to find her own romantic partner, instead of allowing her guardians to choose a suitable spouse, continues to be seen as a threat to established structures. Even today, women who dare to defy patriarchal norms are taunted, ostracized, attacked and killed in the name of 'honour'. There is no honour involved. It is once again, a patriarchal opposition to the sexual autonomy and agency of women.

Uttar Pradesh, in the eighteen months from 2017–2019, saw twenty-three 'honour' killings, with the woman and/or her 'lower' caste partner being killed (Indo-Asian News Service, 2019). A chilling documentary on socially accepted forms of rape in Haryana by news channel *The Quint* ('Rape is consensual', 2018) showed a young boy, barely twelve years old, boldly stating that women needed to stay at home and not go out. A Haryana Khap Panchayat banned girls older than ten from wearing jeans and carrying mobile phones, insisting these two factors would lead to crimes against girls and women.

It comes as no surprise therefore that wife-beating is common nationwide. According to NFHS 4 data, more than half of all women (52 per cent) and men (42 per cent) agreed that it was justifiable for a husband to beat his wife under some circumstances. Women and men most often agreed that wife-beating was justified when the wife disrespected her in-laws or neglected the home or children.

Acid attacks are also becoming a common form of revenge among stalkers whose advances have been spurned by the girls they harassed. A girl being stalked often does not tell her parents about it, because her father or older brothers may punish her for inviting male attention. Her stalker punishes her for spurning him, and she has nowhere to turn. An article in *India Today* (Roy, 2020) states that National Crime Records Bureau (NCRB) data revealed '1,483 victims of acid attacks in the country, between 2014 and 2018,' and that 'out of 523 cases which went for trial, only 19 ended in conviction.'

An even newer version of the deterrence strategy plays itself out on social media. Outspoken women are routinely trolled on Twitter with threats of rape, killing and molestation. A report by Amnesty International in 2019, found that one in seven tweets about women politicians were problematic and abusive. Women politicians in India received more online abuse than their counterparts in the United Kingdom (UK) and the United States of America (USA). This had the effect of silencing some of them and deterring women on the whole from entering politics or claiming leadership positions. A new study shows the shocking scale of abuse on Twitter against women politicians in India (Amnesty International 23 January 2020).

As I write this, a YouTuber called Shubham Mishra has made obscene rape threats against a woman and uploaded the video quite brazenly on social media. The woman, Agrima Joshua, is a stand-up comic and had joked about a statue of Chhatrapati Shivaji (Shukla 2020). Journalist Rana Ayyub has received death and rape threats on her Twitter feed for speaking out about the problems in Kashmir.

For women it is a choice between speaking up and staying safe—even in the online space.

4. Divide

Kaikeyi vs Kaushalya, Sita vs Shoorpanakha, Satyabhama vs Rukmini, Draupadi vs Subhadra, Devyani vs Sharmishtha, and mother-in-law vs daughter-in-law—our history and mythology is replete with stories of rivalries between women. There are few references of women actively supporting other women or women nurturing friendships with women. The 'sakhi' or female friend in Indian dances and literature is only a channel for the heroine to voice her yearning for the hero. At best, these friends tease the heroine and provide us with light-hearted entertainment. In Rabindranath Tagore's 1903 novel *Chokher Bali*, the two women friends use the term 'eyesore' or 'irritant in the eye' to describe their friendship. So it has been with most women as they focus on earning the attention, protection and love of the man.

The fourth and most insidious strategy to keep women from power is to divide them by using collusion. The divide-and-rule strategy has a long history, having been adopted by colonial powers and conquering nations to split the oppressed population and forestall any attempt at revolution. The British inducted a large number of Indian soldiers into their army and English-speaking clerks into their administration, who enforced the law on behalf of their masters. The divide between those who speak English and those who don't still exists as a social marker of class in India today.

Over the centuries, most women have been co-opted into patriarchy and unknowingly collude with it to perpetuate its customs and norms in the name of tradition and culture. The message is so clear and so powerful that it has stood the test of time. The popular media also does its bit with every other popular television serial and soap opera pitting one woman (the 'good girl') against another (the 'evil vamp').

In every workshop that I do with women, a majority agree that women are the first to judge and gossip about other women. Little knowing that in doing so, they are becoming the watchdogs of patriarchy. Other ways of collusion include adopting 'masculine' trappings—smoking and drinking with the boys, being aggressive, swearing freely and looking down on other women who are 'typical women'. The 'typical women' in turn spurn and deride the 'bitch'. There is no victory for either of them.

These four strategies—diminish, decorate, deter, divide—have worked extremely well in keeping women from both personal and positional power.

Centuries of systemic oppression has deprived women of agency. We cannot ignore the external milieu or the existing unfair power structures. Yes, there needs to be social, economic and political change. But changing laws alone cannot change mindsets hardened over thousands of years. Yes, men need to change their mindsets and behaviors as well. But for women, the unlocking has to start from within. We cannot buy into the narrative of women as weak powerless beings and then expect the 'system' to empower us or endow us with special privileges. To begin with, we need to redefine power.

Dacher Keltner in his book *The Power Paradox* found that the widespread tendency has been to think of power as involving extraordinary acts of coercive force. But this definition does not make sense of the great social changes in human history.

Mary Beard, the author of *Women and Power* (2017), defines power as the ability to be effective, to make a difference in the world and the right to be taken seriously—together, as much as individually. Beard writes, 'You cannot easily fit women into a structure that is already coded as male; you have to change the structure. That means thinking about power differently … It means, above all, thinking of power as an attribute or even a verb ("to power"), not as a possession.'

Martin Luther King, in his historic speech 'Where do we go from here?' (n.a.) said, 'power properly understood, is nothing but the ability to achieve purpose.'

I see power as wholehearted 'be-ing'—fully living in our own essence, honouring the wonderful uniqueness in us and integrating the energies for our growth. Then, we need to seek to identify and claim our power. It is only be accessing our inner power that we can exert power in the outer world. This can happen only if we know ourselves well and can awaken the slumbering powers within us—qualities that we have kept locked-up, skills that we have disowned. This will happen if we can see the unloved, broken and hidden parts of ourselves and bring them into the light. We need to own our radiance and our darkness to feel whole and complete. We cannot always do this on our own. All of us need some help and some guidance to help us reach our destination.

This is what I hope to provide through this book.

3

The Six Sources of Power

Remember Indian movies from a decade ago, or even today? Not much has changed. There is the hero (who fights against evil and takes revenge), the heroine (the good girl), the wicked male villain and the female vamp (both of whom usually die, or are arrested at the end), the widowed long-suffering mother, the loyal (male) friend always by the hero's side, and finally, the wise elder. All of these are archetypes in their full glory. We buy into them and believe in them. Our lives are governed at a subtle level through these unconscious images, patterns and symbols.

While we all have our own personalities (based on genetics and personal experiences), there is a deeper subconscious pattern that plays out in each life—a kind of a universal template that impacts our energy and power, and thus shapes how we perceive and interact with the world.

The Archetypes and the Collective Unconscious (1991), Carl Gustav Jung's seminal work, brought the discussion on archetypes and human psychology to the fore. Archetypes are fundamental structures of the psyche. They exist in the collective unconscious and are encoded into the human brain. We can spot these patterns everywhere, even in the gender socialization that occurs in every society as children grow up. These days baby girls are dressed in pink and boys in blue. Girls are given dolls to play with, while boys play with fire trucks. Both boys and girls are told how to behave and what is expected from them. Socialization happens through storytelling, role modelling and enforcement of gendered norms by the authorities—parents, teachers and elders. Myths and stories carry strong messages that reinforce the dominant narrative in society. Boys don't cry. Girls can't shout. This coding lasts a lifetime.

There are symbols and stories of the archetypes all around us. They are also to be found in ancient literature, and in myths and stories that have been passed on through the ages. As Masimilla Harris and Bud Harris state in their work *Into the Heart of the Feminine* (2015):

> Every culture since the beginning of time has existed on its stories. These old myths and tales reflect the structures of our lives today. And they describe how the energies of life, our archetypal patterns are living through us. Examining them teaches us about intimacy with ourselves: how we are structured and how we can accept that we must face seemingly insoluble problems, unbearable realities and the nature of our deepest longings.

I became fascinated by the archetypes when I encountered them in the course of my leadership-development work. In this book, I use the archetypes as sources of power. They are in some ways like battery packs that run us, giving us energy. Sometimes they get drained and need to be recharged. If we identify and use them well, these power sources will help us be fully experienced and express our own power. I use archetypes in workshops to help people identify their archetypes and deepen personal awareness.

Feminine Archetypes and Modern Identity

Shakespeare spoke of the seven ages of man (not woman) in his play *As You Like It*—the mewling infant, the schoolboy, the lover, the soldier, the middle-aged man (he refers to this period as 'the justice, in fair round belly', the age when a man enjoys the fruit of his labours), and finally the decrepit old man sans teeth, sans eyes, sans taste, sans everything. John Eldredge's *The Way of the Wild Heart* (2006) is about the six stages of a man's journey—from a beloved son to a sage.

Hindu dharma only mentions the four stages of life that a man must go through—'brahmacharya', as the celibate student; 'grihastha', as the householder; 'vanaprastha', when (having completed his duties in the preceding stages) he must abandon worldly life and head-off to live in the forest; and finally 'sanyasa' or renunciation, when he becomes a recluse seeking divine union. The unwritten rule for a woman is to live in her father's house until married, and thereafter to accompany her husband through the last three stages of his life.

The only clear distinction between female types (and not female archetypes) is found in an arcane eleventh-century sex manual called *Ratirahasya* (1965), written by Pandit Kokokka. He categorizes women as Padmini (the lotus-like woman), Chitrini (the woman who looks like a work of art), Shankini (the woman who resembles a shell) and Hastini (the elephant-like woman). This classification is based more on physical features, appearance and sexual appeal, than on any great psychological insights. Shankini, for example, 'is warm, well-built with big breasts and firm waist. Her skin is most often white. Her head, hands and feet are larger and her voice is hoarse. She is moody, changing, and violent, subject to attacks of passion.'

These women seem to belong to the pages of a book rather than to real life. Nevertheless, all these works are historical precedents that link the stages in a woman's life not to role changes (as with men), but to her own biological changes—infancy, puberty (daughter stage), pregnancy, menopause and post menopause (wife and later widow stage). She is staged as one of the props in a man's life, though men play lead roles in her life. She doesn't get to play the lead even in her own life.

Many centuries after these epics and other historical works were written, when I began my work with archetypes, there were still very few women in senior positions of power, so most of the participants in my workshops were men. Robert Moore and Douglas Gillette's 1992 work *King, Warrior, Magician, Lover* familiarized me with the male archetypes (lover, warrior, king and magician) and I found them useful in my work. However, as the number of women attending my workshops increased over time, I began to notice differences in the archetypal energies in women, as compared to men.

Women spoke about guilt and shame. Women felt powerless more often than men. Women were afraid of their own power and freedom. I sensed suppressed rage and resentment. Motherhood was a strong theme. And so I began exploring the female archetypes, starting with Jung who spoke of the anima and animus, the feminine and masculine aspects of the psyche. Every man is supposed to have an anima (an unconscious feminine side) and every woman, an animus (a masculine aspect). Jung did a lot of work on anima in the man—identifying the four aspects as Eve, Helen, Mary and Sophia—but did not bother too much about the woman's animus.

Jungian analyses still uses variations of the male archetype—lover, warrior, mother, and high priestess—for female archetypes. These have been further explored by several psychologists, including by Jean Shinoda Bolen who examines female archetypes in her book *Goddesses in Everywoman* (2004). All of these works however reference Western myths, and so I ended up reading books about Greek goddesses and their energies. Each drew her power from her core energy, her essence. Demeter was the mother goddess, Persephone, the innocent persecuted maiden, and Athena, the warrior.

The Western narrative of archetypes was all quite fascinating, but somehow I could not connect to the stories of Hera, Persephone and Aphrodite. They seemed too remote and distant from my everyday life. I had grown up with Lakshmi, Parvati, Saraswati and Durga. These were my goddesses. I still prayed to them. Around this time, I also read more of Hindu mythology, having been exposed to the two favourite and timeless epics right from childhood. I had heard the Ramayan from my grandmother. I have told it to my daughter, who also loved the animated version of the story. The many versions of the Mahabharat and Ramayan have been the most popular of all television serials in India. I remember how we used to be glued to the screen watching Ramanand Sagar's *Ramayana*. We all knew the story. We knew everything about the characters. There was no suspense. Still we were drawn to it again and again.

These were the stories from where we drew our energy. These were the inspirations of the female power in our culture. Sita, Kaushalya, Kaikeyi, Shoorpanakha and Mandodari, each had a distinct pattern. Draupadi, Kunti, Gandhari and Saytavati were complex characters, who each had a unique story. These archetypes are deeply etched in our consciousness. These stories were also the sources of the narratives and patterns embedded in our collective unconscious. I read the more modern versions of the Ramayan and Mahabharat—including Chitra Banerjee Divakaruni's *The Palace of Illusions* (2008) and *Forest of Enchantments* (2019), which gave us Draupadi's version of the Mahabharat, and Sita's version of the Ramayan, respectively; and Amish Tripathi's new spin to the old story of Sita, by portraying her as the *Warrior of Mithila* in his book by the same name (Tripathi, 2017).

Nevertheless, the image of Sita—a chaste, virtuous woman, badly treated by the world—is the predominant narrative and the archetype that still holds. I recently watched a short video clip by Apurva Purohit, an author and the president of Jagran Prakasan, where she exhorted women not to be 'suffering Sitas'.

In the course of my work I saw all these feminine archetype energies and patterns in the women I coached and interacted with. We drew inspiration from some of the stories, others limited our growth. I saw how energy imbalances created behavioural patterns that fail to serve us—too little of an archetype energy leaves us weakened, powerless, feeling blocked, feeling guilt, shame, anger, sorrow and/or fear; an overabundance of it and we behave in a destructive, cruel, cold and disconnected manner.

I realized that when we are truly in balance, our full power emerges and we experience flow, joy, creativity and contribution. We are the best versions of ourselves. This is a heady feeling.

Through the course of my work with women, I identified six feminine archetypes. I call this the Six Feminine Powers Model. Each archetype is an energy or power which can be harnessed by us and used for our growth. These archetypes are universal, though their cultural coding and endorsement is particular to Indian women (I share the coding for each archetype in subsequent chapters).

These six archetypes are evident when viewed through the lens of age, biological and psychological development; these powers are also the ways in which a woman discovers and lives her true potential.

The stages of growth as we come into our full power are not linear. Archetypal energies can show up at any stage in our life. However, there are certain phases in our life when a particular archetypal energy is the most obvious, prevalent and often needed as well. With each archetype I also share the example of a woman who has continued to embody its energy much after the 'onset' years; and often archetypes may overlap in a woman's life, as you will see.

The Kanya Archetype

This archetype embodies innocence and play. The Kanya energy flows fully for a daughter who is cherished and loved by her parents. She learns the rules of the world, what is acceptable and what is not. She wants approval and love from her parents and friends. She develops her own moral compass. She is the typical 'good girl', the nice 'girl next door' whom we all love.

Though Kanya energy is often seen in young girls, many women retain this youthful energy and a sense of innocent mischief well into later years as well. Hindi film-actress Juhi Chawla, for instance, continues to exude a youthful, innocent Kanya energy even in her fifties. She can play many roles, but is easiest and most natural as the nice girl next door. She has a tinkling laugh and her eyes have a mischevious twinkle even today. She will probably carry this Kanya energy through her life.

The Apsara Archetype

The Apsara energy becomes obvious when a girl becomes aware of her body and her identity as separate from that of her parents. It is usually marked by the onset of menses and is traditionally referred to as 'coming of age'. The girl spends more time in front of the mirror, becomes interested in her looks, and experiences an increased awareness of the opposite sex. The young Apsara in her full power is a charming girl, aware of her attractiveness. She is eager to explore her sexuality and begins to realize that this can be a source of power.

Apsaras in their full power are always sensual and charming. Actresses like Katrina Kaif and Malaika Arora continue to exude the Apsara power well into their adult years, are effortlessly sensual and are seen as the epitome of feminine beauty. Another example would be the actress Madhubala, who passed away in 1969, but is still considered a great beauty.

The Veera Archetype

The Veera is full of warrior energy, ready to take charge of her life. In Western cultures, this stage is marked by sending boys and girls out of the home to college or to earn a living, to face the world, face their own struggles and embark on the next stage of the journey of life. This is the time when a young woman makes her own decisions and charts the course of her life. If there are restrictions, she summons up the energy to fight them. She often does not follow the prescribed norms and charts her own destiny. A Veera, who has an excess of this energy, is often seen as 'crazy' by those who cannot understand her fiery, disruptive energy. The Veera usually does not really care what others think about her and this aspect becomes a source of power for her in a world where most women are restricted by the notion of 'what will people say'.

Actress Kangana Ranaut, now in her mid-thirties, embodies the Veera energy. She left home against her parents' wishes to become a model in Delhi. She describes herself as someone who rebelled against the patriarchy in her household. She continues to be seen as a non-conformist who makes her own rules, often speaking out against the established system.

The Rani Archetype

The Rani wants stability, order and a space to call her own. The Rani represents a young woman who is ready for companionship and is willing to 'settle down' (as entering the married state, as is referred to in India). Both sexes are supposed to 'settle down', but the Indian society would like the woman to do it sooner. The phrase 'settle down' implies a more mature, grounded sedate energy. After marriage, a woman enters a new home and makes it her own. She also settles into her life path. In a typical Indian joint family the presence of a senior Rani, in the form of the mother-in-law, can prevent the new bride from truly expressing her own new-found Rani energy.

Once in her full power, the Rani is in control of her destiny and surroundings, and exudes contentment and connection. The popular actress Madhuri Dixit ruled the Bollywood screen in the eighties and nineties. In 1999, she decided to get married to a man chosen by her parents. She was ready to settle down and find companionship and contentment. She moved to Los Angeles, away from the spotlight, and focused on her home, her husband, and later on her children. Now in her mid-fifties, she exudes a regal Rani energy, that of a woman who is comfortable and secure.

The Ma Archetype

The Ma has the energy of nourishment , empathy and concern for others. This archetype embodies the desire to create new life and provide it with nurture and care. The Ma is naturally caring, bountiful, patient and self-sacrificing.

Many women have maternal instincts from an early age while others don't fully develop it at any stage. There is enormous social pressure on women to become mothers, ideally as early as possible after marriage. The birth of a child is definitely a complete change for most people and the beginning of a new phase of life. Motherhood has been exalted to a noble virtue but many women can be biological mothers without fully embodying the Ma archetype.

The actress who played the typical Indian mother, more often than any other actress of her time, was the late Nirupa Roy. Though I do not know how she was as a mother outside the silver screen, her on-screen persona epitomized everything about the Ma archetype. She always put her children first, she loved them and scolded them, she sacrificed everything for them and kept them on the path of goodness and virtue.

The Rishika Archetype

The Rishika archetype is embodied by the qualities of maturity, intelligence and wisdom. This is often seen in the post-menopausal woman who is rich with the wisdom of the years that have gone by. She wants to devote her time and energy to intellectual and spiritual pursuits. She is a natural teacher and mentor. Others turn to her for advice. She experiences a new kind of freedom and space. In traditional Indian households, this is the time when women become more religious, attend religious meetings and spend more time in places of worship and ashrams. The Rishika energy exudes gravitas and seriousness. She wants to serve a greater cause.

Actress Aparna Sen, now in her seventies, has a strong Rishika energy. After starting out as an actress, she became a director and producer. She was also the editor of a women's magazine. She has a wide range of intellectual pursuits and addresses social causes in her films. Her serious, bespectacled demeanour and constant desire to learn reveals that she has transitioned to the role of a Rishika effortlessly.

Invoking the Power of the Archetypes

These six power-archetypes are inherent in all of us. We do experience all the powers at some point in our efforts to move towards wholeness and fulfilment. Women who do not marry or have children can and do invoke the energies of the Rani and Ma in other aspects of their lives. The single woman can find great contentment in having a home and a space where she feels secure, with a pet or parent. A woman who is not a biological mother can invoke the Ma energy to create new works of art, or projects, or express Ma energy in the way she relates to her team. I know of a woman who is not a mother, but is passionate about gardening and reforestation. This is her way of nurturing new life. Many women who have bypassed the Apsara in their teens find her later in life, by taking care of their body and looks.

If we know the energies that reside in us, we can harness them and use them wisely. We can make better choices, have more fulfilling relationships and fulfil our potential. If we are unable to channel them well or use them in the wrong context, they can drain and defeat us. While aspects of all archetypes are inherent in us, some are more dominant than the others. Some remain latent. Some have served us well at a particular stage/context in life but could fail us in another context at another time.

The objective of learning about our archetypes is not to become the perfect embodiment of all six. We cannot, even if we want to. Most women have one or two dominant archetypes, with the others being invoked, depending on situation and context. The idea is to invoke the right energy at the right time, even as we stay true to who we are.

No single archetype is more powerful than the other. Every archetype has a unique power and an important role in our life. In India, we know this almost intuitively and the practice of invoking different energies is a part of our culture. Hindus pray to the goddess Lakshmi when seeking wealth and prosperity. In north India, no Diwali is complete without a Lakshmi Pooja. Students pray to Saraswati, the goddess of knowledge, before exams. The Durga Pooja celebrations invoke the power of the goddess Durga in all her glory. There are even myths that if we upset gods and goddesses, they can strike us down with diseases and have to be pacified through prayer and ritual for the disease to depart.

Feminine energy is not about suppressing masculine energy and wholeness comes with the integration of the two. Lord Vishnu needed to become the beautiful Mohini to get the nectar from the Asuras. The demon Mahishasur could not be killed by any man, so the gods invoked the feminine Shakti and created Durga. Mohini and Durga are both derived from masculine divinities, yet are greater than them. Similarly, all archetypal energies, whether we call them masculine or feminine, reside within each of us. Each of us has the power to cure ourselves. The gods live in each of us, in all of us.

The archetypes embody aspects of our authentic self.

The Persona and the Authentic Self

All of us have a part of us that is 'the persona', the mask we wear, the face we show to the world. The persona is adopted for workability and to get our needs met. Sometimes, the world can see through the mask, sometimes it fits us so well that it makes us look naturally good. People adopt a persona that helps them manage a phase of life or a situation, but that is not the real essence of who they are. Draupadi, the Pandava queen, tried to be an obedient daughter-in-law and a good wife to her five husbands, but at her core she was a Veera-driven—determined, angry and seeking blood-thirsty revenge.

People in the public eye adopt a persona that works for them. If they need to get things done, they have to behave in a certain way. The late J. Jayalalithaa, an actress who eventually took to politics and became the chief minister of Tamil Nadu, took on the Ma persona when she came into politics. The Apsara persona of her glamour years as an actress would not serve her well in her new role.

True power lies in integration and the ability to summon the right energy when it is the right time for it. It is dangerous to identify too closely with the persona and spend a lot of energy being who you are not. This cannot be sustained for long.

The Shadow

The shadow aspect of our psyche is that part of us which we don't own or acknowledge, simply because we don't know it exists and is part of who we are. We have shut it away because we believe it is not welcome or accepted by others.

The shadow is not a harmful energy but is more like a wounded child. We know we are encountering our shadow when we react violently—with judgement, hatred, fear or condemnation—towards someone who displays the traits of our shadow. For a long time, I had a strong judgement against women who dressed in a showy or provocative way. Bright red lipstick and long shiny nails would send a shudder through my body. I would feel very uncomfortable when I saw scenes in movies where women seduced men and expressed their desire openly. After understanding more about my shadow, I realized that the Apsara was my shadow and my repudiation of this aspect showed up in these encounters.

Knowing the energy sources and blocks helps us to navigate life better. Ultimately, our goal is to move towards wholeness and flow. Jung called this individuation, self-actualization through integration of the conscious and unconscious. My way of looking at it is to be the best version of yourself so that you can make choices that best serve you and the community. Your persona is acknowledged and shadow beautifully integrated, and you show up fully for who you are.

I have examined my own life-pattern using the archetypes and found it immensely useful. I hold both the Kanya and Rishika powers. I have been (and am still) a Kanya, the archetypal good girl, the nice girl. I was an obedient daughter who rarely broke rules. I did very well at school. It was important for me to stand first, because academic success got me acceptance from my family. I recall being very upset when the first rank medal was taken away from me and given to another girl. I had come second and had to give up the coveted medal. I was in Class II! The Kanya energy ensures that I am pleasant, compliant and driven to do well.

Damayanthi, the heroine of my first novel *Keep the Change* (2010), is a typical Kanya. I drew upon some of my experiences and feelings to create her character. Damayanthi admits, 'I am not a woman who runs with the wolves. I am more of the woman who ambles home with the cows.' It is only when she harnesses her warrior energy and takes the step of moving away from her home to a new, unknown city that she comes into her own. She faces betrayal and failure and is able to manage difficult situations by invoking her other energies. Damayanthi does not stop being the Kanya, but she is able to be much more.

Another energy I recognize in myself is that of the Rishika, the wise seeker. I love reading and the acquisition of knowledge. I have been described as calm, centred and mature for my age. Over the last decade, the Rishika power has guided me on the path of greater self-awareness and spirituality. The Rishika also keeps me a little distant and disconnected from others. I have received feedback from my colleagues that I sometimes seem a little remote, 'lost in my ivory tower'.

The Kanya and Rishika energies have been sources of power as I pursue the path of learning and contribution. The Kanya has kept me safe. The Rishika has kept me sane. However, when I attended a Gender and Identity Lab, I realized that there was a disconnection from my body and some shame around my sexuality. The Apsara had been dormant and shut-off. I now realize that my second novel *Intermission* (2012) was about the expression of the Apsara energy.

Both the female characters in that book—Sweety Singh and Gayatri Sarin—are initially not able to express the Apsara energies fully. Sweety, the Kanya, discovers her inner Apsara in an extramarital affair. Gayatri, the Rani, is frustrated in her marriage and tries to distract herself through massages, training sessions and her work.

I grew up thinking that beauty and sexuality were 'bad', because they earned me unwanted attention from men and kept me from my goals. I recall once when I was fifteen, a boy called my home on the only phone we had—a landline. I received a 'talking to' from my mother and felt ashamed and guilty for encouraging this attention. In my typical Tamil Brahmin family, simplicity and intellectual pursuits were encouraged more than ostentation and artistic tendencies. In later life, I needed to invoke and access my Apsara energies for greater self-expression and a better connection with my partner. I have started taking some steps in that direction. I enjoy the 'shringar', the process of dressing up rather than seeing it as a chore I need to perform. I am not very fond of jewellery, but when my friend Rhea gave me a nose ring to invoke my Apsara, I felt something shift in me. I saw myself in a different way with that small addition. I now often wear a nose ring and feel more connected to my sensuality.

Another energy I need to invoke was the Veera energy. I wanted to grow my work and amplify my impact, but was hesitant about marketing and personal branding. I held on to the beliefs I had grown up with. *Girls need to be modest. Talking about your work is boasting. There is something sleazy about marketing yourself.*

I would wait for work to come to me believing that if I kept my head down and did a good job, clients would automatically find me. I saw people, who in my opinion were not as experienced or qualified as I was, doing more work and demanding higher fees. I had to summon my courage and start putting myself out there. I started writing more regularly on social media. I told people about the work I did. I went from 'I do some training', to 'I have my own organization and specialize in people-development solutions'.

Identifying the specific sources and putting in practices to overcome power blocks has helped me achieve my goals. I feel better. I feel powerful and in charge of my life. When I am in my full power, I connect better to the world around me and have a more powerful impact. Power is not something to be grabbed from another person. It is something to be sourced from within ourselves. We have all the resources we need. My intention is to use this work to give women an access to identify and claim their power.

When we know about our archetypal power, own and claim it fully, and are able to invoke other powers as needed, we find joy, purpose and flow. Each power has a positive side and a negative side. An over-development of one archetypal energy leads to power blocks. We begin to show our worst side and we lose sight of the positive aspect of our unique power. We tend to rely too heavily only on one power which defines and shapes our whole self.

The next six chapters are about each of the archetypes. So, read about each archetype and find yourself in them. You may connect to more than one archetype. You may find a mix of two or three in yourself. Allow yourself to read about all of them first. Understand the bright side of each power and the blocks to power. If any archetype evokes strong feelings of 'This is totally not like me' or 'I can't stand women like these', you are probably encountering your shadow—an undeveloped aspect of yourself. In each chapter, I also share the pathway to growth if you are facing power blocks. Growth will also happen when you integrate your shadow power. Then read the last two chapters (Chapter 10 'The Journey to Becoming Powerful', and Chapter 11 'Practices to Invoke Your Power') for how you can realize your true power. Chapter 11 offers you practices and simple solutions to evoke each archetype when needed. The chapter 'Powers at a Glance' provides you with a ready-reckoner table that highlights aspects of each of the six power archetypes. You can also take the Powerfulife Assessment first to get your power profile at www.powerfulife.in. Then read this book to interpret your profile and get some insights for your growth.

I have also shared some case studies. These are based on the coaching sessions I have done with women, examples shared during workshops and stories I have heard from the women during conversations. The names and some details have been changed to protect their identities but the situations are real and relevant.

4
Kanya: The Good Girl

The Aranya Kand in the Valmiki Ramayan states: 'Kaamavratam idam raudram streenaam asadrisham matam' (It is not desirable for a woman to be self-seeking). This is could well describe the Kanya—the virtuous maiden, the good girl—a recurrent motif in almost all our stories. The innocent maiden is the heroine of all fairy tales. She goes through trials and tribulations but triumphs over them and is rewarded with a happily-ever-after.

The Kanya is the most common archetype seen in Indian women, since it has received strong cultural endorsement over the ages. The Kanya leads a sheltered life, protected by her parents. Her childhood is unmarked by great sorrow or great joy. She takes pleasure in the simple things of life. Mostly, she wants to please her parents and make them proud of her. She does this by being good and obeying them. She may secretly envy rebellious girls, but she does not want to be like them and get scolded. She has a good group of friends, who are mostly like her. The Kanya may giggle in class, but never so loudly as to draw punishment from the teacher. She may sometimes gossip about bad girls who get into trouble. The Kanya usually avoids trouble and restricts herself to harmless pranks. Nothing pleases her more than an affectionate look from her mother, an approving nod from her father.

The Kanya who receives the nurture and affection she wants, grows up to be a confident happy young woman. She is secure in her self-worth and will try to create a harmonious environment wherever she is, as she likes ease and comfort. At her best, the Kanya is a charming, light-hearted, easygoing woman who just wants to live and let live.

The Kanya tends to believe that the world is a good place and trusts easily. Her ability to retain this optimistic view in times of trouble is one of her key strengths. Others may see her as a little naïve but she believes in her ideals, is dependable and comes through for her near and dear ones. Pleasant, soft-spoken and open in her conversations, the Kanya is careful not to give offence and can move from spontaneity to diplomacy, depending upon the circumstances. She is flexible and will adapt easily to her circumstances. People like having the Kanya around.

The Kanya also has a strong moral core. Lying and cheating do not come easily to her. She is prone to be proper. She follows the rules that she believes are required for a moral order in the world. Do not mistake her compliance for blind obedience. She will fight for what she believes is right, but she will usually avoid conflict.

The 'kanyadan' is a common ritual in our weddings, when the Kanya is literally given away ('dan') by her owner (the father) to the new owner (the husband). The kanyadan marks the end of the young virgin maiden and the beginning of the chaste wife or the mature Kanya. The three knots (or *moondru mudhichu* as we say in Tamil) to tie the scared thread around her neck during the ceremony are the ties that bind her to the new role and family.

Something happens to the Kanya when she dons the red sindoor, the mangalsutra and the wedding sari. Though she still retains the desire for love and acceptance, and is still the trusting optimist who tries to see the best in everyone, her main desire now is not to find a man to love, but to preserve the relationships in her new home. Sex is primarily for procreation or for pleasing the husband. She is not expected to demand it or derive pleasure from it. She gracefully segues from being the good daughter to being the good daughter-in-law and wife so that she might live out the rest of her life in peace and quiet joy.

Many Kanyas retain a girlish quality even as they age. They giggle like young girls and dress younger than their age. Preserving this youthful quality is important to them. They play the role of the dutiful daughter and wife, but in the company of other women, in safe spaces, they let their hair down and have a good time. They do not brood or think too deeply. 'Live in the present and be pleasant' is their motto.

Kanya's Cultural Coding

The Kanya is seen as the ideal woman in our culture. The preservation of virginity or innocence and the degradation that follows its loss is a recurring motif in ancient and modern stories. Even in contemporary India, a woman's virginity is equated with her morality. In Tamil, the colloquial term for being raped (*kettu poita*) is the same as spoiled or soiled. A woman who has lost this aspect that denotes her innocence is sinful and corrupt.

Virginity is thus a precious commodity, to be guarded and preserved until it is claimed by the rightful owner. This notion cuts across religions and cultures. From the Virgin Mary in Christianity, to the promise of seventy-two virgins in heaven in Islam, chaste women are prized everywhere. Losing one's virginity before marriage is sinful and shameful, and the wayward Kanya may be punished with an unwanted pregnancy, ostracization and all kinds of sorrows before she realizes the error of her ways.

In the Hindi film *Julie* (1975), based on the Malayalam film *Chattakari* (The Anglo-Indian Girl; 1974), the Anglo-Indian heroine sleeps with her Hindu boyfriend before marriage and becomes pregnant. In the hit Hindi film *Aradhana* (Worship; 1969), the heroine, Vandana, elopes with her lover and has a secret unofficial marriage after which she sleeps with him. Her lover dies and she is left with a baby which she has to give up for adoption. The message: nothing good ever comes of losing your virginity before a legal and social union.

While most contemporary films do show heroines engaging in guiltless premarital sex without any repercussions, a 2019 Sex survey by the magazine *India Today* showed that 53 per cent of respondents believed that a woman's virginity was still an important issue in the relationship.

In the short film *Leeches* (2016), a young Muslim girl, Zainab is sold as a bride for a day to a rich old man who values her virginity. Her older sister wants to protect her and resorts to a painful old remedy involving leeches so that Zainab can fake her virginity. This practice of valuing and seeking only virgin brides is still prevalent in India.

The ability to restore one's virginity is a superpower referred to in mythology. In the Mahabharat, Draupadi is the wife of all five Pandava brothers, though this was a time when polyandry was not prevalent. She received a boon that her virginity would be restored every morning after her sexual encounters with each husband. That way, each man would get a virgin bride!

After marriage, the virgin bride becomes the chaste wife.

Sita, in the Ramayan, is the archetypal Kanya. She is the beloved daughter of her father, King Janaka, and is nurtured by her parents so that she becomes a confident, loving woman. She eases smoothly into married life, winning the approval and affection of her mother-in-law, Kaushalya. She is the devoted wife, who follows her husband into the forest. But Sita does have a childish wilful streak: she demands that her husband bring her a golden deer which she had fleetingly spotted in the forest. The events that ensue show that she is of course punished by the fates for such self-seeking behaviour—Ravan kidnaps her.

In all versions of the Ramayan, Sita preserves her chastity even after being kidnapped. However, her husband refuses to her take back. He has fought the battle not for her but for the sake of his honour. In the Ramayan (Yuddha Kand, Sarga 115) he says to her, 'You, with a suspicion arisen on your character, standing in front of me, are extremely disagreeable to me, even as a light to one, who suffers from a poor eyesight.'

Despite being a good, virtuous wife, Sita is rejected by her husband who fears public scandal and aspersions on his noble lineage. Sita proves herself by taking the *agni pariksha* or trial by fire, walks through fire and comes out unscathed. This proves her innocence and she is accepted, only to be cast out again later when Rama comes to know that a common citizen has cast aspersions on Sita's purity. Kanyas are driven to constantly prove their goodness and innocence. Sita, Anusuya, Ahalya, and Savitri are all Kanyas who are revered as virtuous wives.

The stories of beloved daughters are few.

According to the Brahma Purana, the first woman, Shatarupa, was created by Brahma who fell in love with his creation. He was so infatuated with her that he sprouted four heads to follow her wherever she went. A nuanced reading of the Puranas is required to understand the true nature of Brahma's relationship with his daughter but the version that holds sway over popular imagination is that of an unhealthy incestuous attraction between a father and his daughter.

After reading Sudha Murty's *The Daughter from a Wishing Tree: Unusual Tales from Indian Mythology*, I came to know about Ashokasundari. The goddess Parvati was bored and lonely since her husband was away and she asked the Wishing Tree—Kalpavriksh—for a companion. While the sons of Shiva and Parvati—Ganesha and Kartikeya—are still worshipped all over the country, Ashokasundari has vanished from our memory.

Many daughters have been given away. Ram's sister, Shanta, and Kunti from the Mahabharat were both given away in adoption. Shakuntala was abandoned by her parents and given to a sage. Draupadi emerged, along with her brother, Drishtadyumna, from a sacred fire to which her father, King Drupad, was praying, asking for a boon to defeat his enemy. He soon decided to get her married to Arjun, and acquire him as a son-in-law. Daughters were only as valuable as a means for a strategic alliance.

There are no role models or narratives for nurturing parenting of daughters. Female foeticide and infanticide still occur in many parts of the country. Even educated urban women have shared that there is an expectation to produce male offspring. The recent campaign of Beti Bachao, Beti Padhao (Save the Daughter, Educate the Daughter) was launched to address this deep-rooted issue. There is some good news, as per an article in the *Financial Express*, the sex ratio in Haryana has gone up from 871 girls per 1,000 boys in 2014 to 923 girls per 1,000 boys in 2019, according to the latest census report.

It is ironical that we seek to protect the innocence and virtue of our young girls (Kanyas) while denying them a childhood that will promote and preserve these qualities.

Kanya's Relationships

The Kanya may not have a boyfriend but she dreams of one. He is not one of the boys in her class or in the neighbourhood, but a Great Love. The Kanya fantasizes about the ideal man but somehow stops short of imagining anything sexual with him. The nodding roses and cooing love birds are enough for her. The Kanya can play the flirt or the coquette easily to win the heart of the man she wants. She will rarely make the first move, but will readily reciprocate if the man attempts to woo her. She takes care to dress well for her dates and is eager to make a good impression.

The Kanya often attracts a mature father figure, the man who treats her like his precious princess and pampers her. She is willing to let him take care of her and reciprocates by pleasing him just as a good daughter tries to win the approval of her father. Both may be quite happy in such a relationship for several years. However, if the Kanya tries to 'grow up' and demand freedom, the husband turns into a strict father, curtailing her movements. He also begins to feel insecure at the prospect of his wife leaving him.

Men are attracted to the Kanya thanks to her perceived purity and innocence. She is the sweet girl next door, who seems simple and incorruptible. Her shyness seems endearing. The man is sure his mother will approve of her and is thus quite ready with the offer of marriage.

The Kanya versus the Apsara theme is played out in the Hindi movie *Cocktail* (2012). The playboy hero, Gautam, has to choose between the wild party girl, Veronica, and the demure good girl, Meera. He introduces Meera as his girlfriend since his mother would approve of her. Veronica too tries to change her ways to become the 'good Indian girl' to win her man and his family. But it is the Kanya who triumphs over the Apsara, and the good girl gets the reformed playboy.

Sometimes, because of her trusting nature, the Kanya is seduced by a man who she thinks will meet her needs, but does not. Since her need for love is great, she usually does not lose hope and continues her search for the ideal man, even though her previous experience has not been a positive one.

Another Hindi film, *Bareilly ki Barfi* (Bareilly's Sweets; 2017) shows the heroine, Bitti, pining for the author of a book that she happens to read on a train. The man who could have written such a book is her ideal man, she decides. Bitti, the romantic, begins a correspondence with Pritam Vidrohi, the author she has never met but has fallen in love with.

Bitti's mother is unhappy and furious with the author for 'spoiling her daughter's mind' and refuses to have anything to do with him. Many misunderstandings and mix-ups later, Bitti finally confronts reality and gets her man. Though the man is not perfect, and is a flawed human being, Bitti realizes that she loves him in a way that is different from the dreamy love of the romantic girl reading a book on a train. She is now a mature Kanya.

The mature Kanya is a loving wife and can be spontaneous and fun to be with. She does not mind her husband taking the initiative in sex and often expects it. This is not so much submissiveness as being happy to go with the flow. She takes care to buy gifts for her husband's family and to maintain good relations with them. The extroverted Kanya takes pleasure in organizing family outings so that everyone can have a good time.

Kanya's Career Choices

The Kanya excels in jobs that deal with people, such as marketing, public relations and communication-related jobs. She is great at building an immediate rapport with customers. If the Kanya can develop the ruthlessness needed for hard negotiations and deal closures, she can become a super saleswoman. Goal-driven Kanyas employ a variety of persuasive techniques to win friends and influence people. However, Kanyas also often underestimate themselves and shy away from roles and jobs that seem tough and demanding.

They have a strong creative bent of mind and can become excellent performing artists, if talented. Many talented Kanyas don't live up to their full potential if they don't get the support they require. They thrive on recognition and appreciation, and a generous dose of this helps them to grow in their chosen field. Some Kanyas do live up to expectations, but get married at the cost of their career. They may resent the authority figure in their lives, but don't show it explicitly. Many Kanyas may choose not to work, or have a career, if this is the prevailing norm in their community or social circle. The Kanya who embraces the Ma archetype after the birth of her children may be quite content with the joys of motherhood.

Overall, the Kanya thrives in a supportive workplace where there is contact and communication with others. She works best when the communication is transparent and she feels trusted and safe.

Kanya as a Leader

Though usually not ambitious enough to aspire for a leadership position, the Kanya will willingly accept the responsibility if she feels that she is capable. As a new leader, she tries to perform and please. She wants acceptance and love from all her team members and is usually diplomatic and careful to avoid hurting others. The good girl as a leader is popular and well regarded.

The Kanya leader trusts her team members and sometimes has difficulty keeping non-performers on track. She believes that if she gives instructions and provides a supportive environment, people will perform. She is also worried that she will never be good enough. A vein of anxiety throbs dully beneath her cheerful exterior, but she keeps her doubts to herself.

She dreads a bad word from her boss and will work hard to ensure that she delivers quality work. The Kanya is deeply influenced by a strong boss and will adhere to the requirements made by someone who has greater power. She will stand up to him or her if her values are compromised or her self-esteem violated, but by and large she will accept the word of the person with the greater authority. The Kanya leader must learn to have those courageous conversations, instead of avoiding confrontations. She needs to learn to go deep, get into detail work and enhance her problem-solving abilities.

She must leverage her communication skills to assert her point of view and make those tough calls even at the cost of her popularity. As she grows in confidence, she must also grow in her comfort with power and position. The respected Kanya leader listens to other people's views objectively instead of being hijacked by them.

THE RISE AND RISE OF SMRITI IRANI: THE KANYA AT WORK

At first glance, Union Minister Smriti Irani can pass-off as a typical Indian housewife. Red sindoor gleams brightly on her forehead, a mangalsutra hangs around her neck and she is always draped in saris. Smriti Irani, who played the role of the dutiful daughter-in-law in a TV serial, has been projected as the dutiful daughter-in-law of the nation.

From beauty pageant contestant to television actress, to a minister who defeated Rahul Gandhi in the 2019 Indian elections, Smriti has come a long way. As I follow the trajectory of her life, the pattern of the mature Kanya begins to emerge. She is intelligent, articulate and humble. She always gives credit to the party leader, Narendra Modi. She is usually affable. She can be assertive without being abrasive. She does not actively seek controversy and shies away from being outrageous.

Optics are important for the Kanya. Of course, optics are always important for people in the public eye. Smriti chooses her words and looks with care. She favours bright colours and is always well-groomed. Even when she ticks-off her opponents, it is done with a smile.

A few years ago, there was a huge controversy around Smriti Irani's educational qualifications. She had not completed college but claimed to have a degree, said media reports. Though she has accomplished more than several highly educated people have, it seems to be a sore spot. Perhaps, she still feels the pain of not having the right credentials. Now she makes it a point to mention her humble beginnings. She talks derisively about the elite Khan Market crowd in Delhi. She will spend the rest of her career proving her critics wrong. She will do it pleasantly, with a smile that only hints at the steel inside.

Smriti Irani has been able to stay true to her Kanya, but her success is due to her ability to integrate other energies, especially those of the Rani and Veera to become a leader. She has learnt to be prepared for battle during question hour in parliament and is seen to be ready with facts and figures. She has built a certain gravitas in her presence and now has emerged as a leader who is respected and admired.

Kanya's Power Sources: Goodness, Innocence, Optimism and Flexibility

The Kanya derives her power from her innate goodness and innocence, and the ability to see the good in others. A case in point is the story of Anusuya, the wife of the sage Atri. She is said to have been the epitome of chastity, praised more than the goddesses for her this quality. The envious goddesses sent their husbands, the great gods Shiva, Brahma and Vishnu, to tempt her and break her vow. The best idea that the gods could come up with was to ask her to serve them food in the nude. Anusuya sprinkled holy water on them and turned them into innocent babies. Everyone was awestruck and the goddesses repented their folly. Sati Anusuya, as she was known, also brought the dead back to life and helped to relieve the country from drought by summoning the river Mandakini to provide water. She was a thus a very powerful woman.

Chastity and faithfulness to a partner are virtues that both men and women can aspire to. However, the unfaithful man has never been powerless. In fact, his ability to have multiple female partners has been a sign of strength and power. Indra seduced and raped several women, but still remained the king of the gods. Stories singing the glories of chastity serve only to keep errant wives in check and curtail the sexual freedom of women. They reinforce the tenuous connection between fidelity and female power.

The Kanya's true power of goodness does not come from chastity as much as it does from loyalty. Her loyalty is a source of strength for her family and friends. She is powerful because of a strong moral compass and an innate honesty. This is not her weakness. Her ability to work hard and be sincere is her strength. She quickly earns the trust of others and lives up to their expectations. She uses her likeability to influence others and win them over to her side. People do things for the Kanya simply because they like her.

Kanya's Core Need: Acceptance

The Kanya's core need is acceptance. Her strategy to gain acceptance is to become a nice girl, a likeable person. She needs a nurturing parent or parents to love her and care for her and she will do anything to keep them happy in return. She is neat, responsible and does well in school. She may never shine brightly or stand out, but no one can fault her. She usually receives the Good Conduct Prize, every year.

The need for acceptance ensures that the Kanya identifies an authority figure who gives her the seal of approval. At home, one of the parents, usually the father, becomes the final authority. At school, the Kanya has a teacher who she looks up to and she is often referred to as 'Teacher's Pet'. As the Kanya grows older, the need for acceptance extends to a group of close friends.

The Kanya may rebel against her parents to gain acceptance from her friends, but her rebellion is quiet and under the radar. She may sneak off in the middle of a school-day, or take a furtive swig of alcohol at a party, but she takes care to ensure that she is not discovered.

Her need to please everyone is her undoing. The Kanya believes that she will be accepted only if she is good. This leads to a blocking of her power.

Kanya's Power Blocks

The Kanya is often unable to access her power because of the emotional drain she experiences due to certain mindsets and consequent emotions that block her power. She becomes lost, confused and loses sight of her goodness and self-worth. An overdevelopment of Kanya energy and absence of other energies blocks the Kanya's power. The Kanya's trusting nature makes her gullible and others take advantage of her naivete.

Emotionally Drained by: Shame

The young Kanya who does not receive the acceptance she so badly craved from her parents grows up feeling that she is not good enough. In my experience coaching women, I have seen this limiting belief more often than others. Though the Kanya tries very hard to do well in school, to be the good sister, to take care of the housework and younger siblings, she knows she will never be loved as much as her baby brother. As she grows up, she looks for opportunities to excel in other areas, hoping for the recognition and approval that she longs for. She will avoid anything that might make her look bad or bring shame to her and her family. The Kanya will work hard at everything for external validation and still feel inadequate.

The Kanya is therefore very concerned about the opinions of the rest of the world. Continuous exhortations by her parents of 'what will people say' has sunk into her DNA and she carries this forward to her children. Unfortunately, virtue has never been its own reward. The Kanya often suffers despite her good nature and good intentions. And she does so in silence. Her biggest emotional drain is shame.

'Sharam nahin aati?' (Aren't you ashamed?) is a question girls are often asked. Shame and the desire to avoid it is what keeps the good girls good. Shame is the feeling of hurt and humiliation when you have done something bad or foolish. Nothing can be more mortifying for the Kanya than shame. Our collective consciousness has in fact glorified the feeling of shame as a necessity for a 'good' woman, camouflaging it in the guise of modesty. 'Lajja stree ka gehna hai' (Modesty is a woman's treasure) is a popular saying in north India. The honour of the whole family rests with the girl. If she shames herself, it brings shame to the entire family.

Her body is often a big source of shame. The phrase 'body shaming' was probably invented by women for women. The Kanya will spend a lot of money trying to look beautiful and have the perfect body, but always feel a little unhappy about her appearance.

Shame is a reason why many women don't bring up issues of sexual harassment. Bringing it up suggests somehow that the woman has not been good or virtuous enough to prevent being sexually harassed. No wonder, many victims of harassment wonder if they have somehow brought it upon themselves. They wonder if they inadvertently gave some hint, or some other vibe that they were asking for it. Talking about the whole situation is so shameful that they prefer to suffer in silence. Kanyas who have experienced shame live with a feeling of unworthiness, as though they will never be good enough.

Fears: Rejection

All of us have the fear of rejection. Rejection by a publisher, by a friend, by a loved one or even a stranger can be extremely painful. Studies show that the same parts of the brain get activated when we experience rejection as when we experience physical pain. Not just the Kanya, any person hates being rejected. However, some of us bounce back easily. Some, experienced salespeople for instance, are able to brush it off quickly. But for the Kanya, rejection is the ultimate fear, far scarier than bungee-jumping or snakes.

So the Kanya does everything possible to avoid potential rejection. Her craving for acceptance usually makes her act in such a way to ensure that she or her work will not be rejected. The Kanya has problems asking for help, because she could be rejected. The Veera may not ask for help because she sees as it a sign of weakness, and the Rishika may not ask for help because she sees it as a sign of incompetence; for the Kanya, asking for help is tantamount to asking for rejection—a slap on the face, to be avoided at all costs.

Responds with: Passivity

The Kanya, in her quest for acceptance, can become a submissive people-pleaser. If she is unable to complement her *Kanya* energy with another power that is needed for her to succeed, she becomes weak, gullible and passive.

This aspect of the Kanya can be seen in many contemporary films and books. In best-selling author Preeti Shenoy's *The Rule Breakers* (2018), the protagonist Veda is the archetypal good girl: the dutiful daughter, studious, obedient and loving. However, she is unable to stand up to her father. She agrees to give up her studies and her first love for an arranged marriage. Later, she suffers at the hands of a wrathful mother-in-law and negligent husband, but is unable to exert her agency. She assiduously completes her household chores and studies for exams at the cost of her health and well-being.

This is the story of many Kanyas.

How the Kanya Grows

The Kanya grows not by avoiding suffering but triumphing over it. The Kanya is initiated into transformation through an ordeal. As she goes through the struggle, she emerges stronger and more determined. She matures from a naïve girl to a strong woman, still retaining her faith and virtue. She must make the choice whether to live the rest of her life passively with shame and rejection, or go through it with courage.

The Kanya grows by inviting new experiences and new beginnings once she is no longer bound by other people's opinions of her. She can stand in front of the waves and allow them to wash over her, knowing that she is in her power. Veda, in *The Rule Breakers*, is able to overcome her power blocks by connecting to a purpose and engaging in a new experience with a non-governmental organization (NGO) called Sankalp (meaning determination). Determination is what she needs in life to succeed. She finally speaks up when she is faced with an unjust accusation. She is able to express herself to her father and also sees a change in the relationship with her mother-in-law. It is only by breaking the rules that she finds happiness and wholeness.

Damini, the 1993 Hindi crime drama starring Meenakshi Seshadri, is about a young wife living the ideal life with a loving husband and family. When she witnesses her brother-in-law raping a maid, her life changes forever. She can choose the easy way and listen to her family, thus hushing up the incident, or go against everything she has known and take the matter to the police. She chooses the latter and despite being declared mentally unstable and locked away in an institution, she persists and finally—with the help of a lawyer—gets justice for the poor maid. Before the happy ending, she has to go through her share of suffering, alienation and rejection by her family and husband, the stuff of nightmares for a Kanya.

The biggest act of courage for such a person is to give up her need for acceptance. This is the drug she has been on for a very long time. It goes against her grain to resist the demands of the authority and sacrifice popularity. There will be situations in her life where she will be called to go through just such a trial by fire. This is a test of her strength and resilience. It is the way for her to achieve wholeness and come into her own.

Queen (2014) is another film that shows the growth of the immature Kanya. The heroine, called Rani, is played by actress Kangana Ranaut. Rani is a typical good Punjabi girl looking forward to her wedding with the man she loves, a match that has the blessings of her parents. When her fiancée ditches her just before her wedding, her world is shattered. She gathers herself and sets off on her honeymoon, alone. It turns out to be the adventure of a lifetime for her. This is the classic heroine's journey where Rani returns from her adventure transformed and more in control of her life. Rani faces her fears—loneliness, ignorance, disconnection, helplessness and loss of love—before she grows fully into her power. Many Kanyas go through life without facing their own demons and shying away from growth. They will always have a niggling feeling that they haven't lived to their full potential, but they cannot step out of their comfort zone to take those dangerous first steps. Instead of living in fear, they need to let go of imaginary anxieties to embrace life fully. Most Kanyas need to invoke their shadow powers—Veera, Rani or Apsara. The Veera power will enable them to speak up, speak out, embrace change and set goals. The Rani power will give them the gravitas, maturity and grounded energy to march towards their goals in a disciplined and focused manner. Many Kanyas also need to accept their body and beauty, by awakening their Apsara archetype. This positive acceptance of their physical appearance allows them freedom from shame and enables them to face the world with greater confidence.

When the Kanya integrates the other powers and is able to implement practices to do so, she comes into her full power and is able to achieve her goals without giving up her values.

Case Studies

Pragati

When I first met her in my condominium, Pragati was a beautiful woman who had a body and a life that was enviable. At forty, this mother of two had the flat stomach of a twenty-year-old and flawless skin. She never went anywhere without makeup. She used to complain about every extra inch she put on after a weekend binge. I would often hear her moan about her dark circles and falling hair, and wanted to shake her hard and ask her to stop whining. 'She is being so superficial', I thought.

Pragati was a great cook and a home-based chef with a good set of clients in the neighbourhood. She was usually very prompt with delivery and easily accepted any suggestions from her clients. Some clients would ask for refunds after eating what she had sent. Some demanded extras like chutney and salad for free. Pragati was unable to put her foot down and express her thoughts.

Pragati's husband was often impatient with her, despite her efforts. She felt unappreciated. She tried so hard at everything but still felt unhappy. The more she tried to please others, the less they seemed to appreciate her. She was always busy doing things for others and got nothing in return. After a while, Pragati started looking haggard, losing her zest for life. She began avoiding calls from clients who were 'difficult'.

After some counselling, she was able to see that her fear of judgement and eagerness to please others did not get her the respect and acceptance that she really craved. She became less stressed and more confident about herself. She learnt to put down some healthy boundaries and was able to firmly but respectfully say 'No!'

Kanika

Kanika was a young woman I was coaching, who had problems asking for help. She felt that she could manage everything on her own and worked very hard, putting in late hours figuring everything out in her new job by herself. She did not delegate work at her workplace; at home too, she insisted on doing everything herself. She also insisted that she didn't mind the hard work, but complained it was taking a toll on her health and on time with her family. Kanika thought she was being self-reliant and independent. Yet every time she needed help from someone, her throat would dry up and she would feel her heart beating loudly. She would end up doing the task herself.

On deeper questioning, she narrated a story from her childhood. When she was eight or nine, one evening, she needed help with her Maths homework and called her father for help. Her father was in another room watching a cricket match on television with her brother, and shouted to her that he would come in a few minutes. Though she called him again, he completely forgot about her. She never brought up the subject with him. That incident left a deep impression on her. She felt rejected, that she was not important to him. Little

Kanika swore that she would never put herself in a situation when she would experience the same feeling of rejection again.

Kanika needed to realize that it was her fear of rejection and the old memory of being ignored by her father that led to this behaviour. It was only when Kanika was able to forgive her father that she was released from this old fear. Her growth depended on asking for support and allowing others to help her. She also realized that people liked her and were happy to help her. Even if there was a possibility of refusal, the prospect no longer filled her with dread.

5

Apsara: The Seductive Beauty

The Mahabharat cautions, 'There is no creature more sinful, O son, than women. Woman is a blazing fire. She is the illusion, O king, that daitya Maya [the demon Maya] created. She is the sharp edge of the razor. She is poison. She is a snake. She is, verily, all these united together' (Anusasana Parva, section XL).

The terrified authors were probably referring to the Apsara, a woman who is often irresistible and is usually aware of her beauty and sensuality. The Apsara is naturally charming and easily seductive. She loves to adorn herself and amplify her beauty. She loves the compliments she gets about her looks. She basks in the attention from the opposite sex. She is usually a good dancer, enjoying the moves and sensuality of bodily expression. In mythology, apsaras were the celestial dancers in the court of Indra, the king of gods.

Today the little girl who spends hours in the front of the mirror, wears her mother's makeup and high heels, and is drawn to the sparkly and shiny is an Apsara in the making. The Apsara energy comes into flow when a girl attains puberty and becomes aware of herself as a woman. The young Apsara is an innocent flirt who wants boys to notice her. An older Apsara will consciously and unconsciously attract attention from others. The Apsara wants admiration from both men and women. This does not need to translate into initiation of a sexual encounter. The Apsara is happy just to be the centre of attention and basks in her glory.

Apsaras do not have many girls as close friends. They are distrusted by the Kanyas and the Mas, and dismissed by the Rishikas and Veeras. Many, however, secretly envy them and want to be like them. Most of the Apsaras are unconcerned. They often live in a little celestial world of their own, living by their own rules, their feet never fully on the ground. They do not like to be tied down. They get bored easily and want to move on to the next attractive thing. They flit, they float searching for something elusive and ideal—the perfect love, the perfect life that will match up to them.

Classical Indian literature and art depict the 'ashta nayikas' or the eight types of heroines, in various moods and emotions. The *Natyashastra* by the sage Bharat, describes these heroines in different romantic situations. The full range of these emotions is available to the Apsara—from the eager 'vasakasajjika', the heroine who adorns herself for her beloved, to the 'abhisarika', the heroine who recklessly leaves the confines of her home to search for her beloved on a dark and stormy night. The Apsara too is ruled by the heart and feels that the rules of society don't apply to her, especially in search of love and fulfilment.

The transition from a young girl to an adolescent is marked by ritual and custom in many cultures across the world. While rituals for boys coming of age persist in only a few indigenous tribes now, many girls still go through a rite of passage across the globe when they get their first period. A girl's transition to puberty is considered both sacred and shameful. Among many communities in Tamil Nadu, a grand celebration is held. I visited my neighbour's daughter's 'vayasakku vandachu', the coming-of-age ceremony. The young girl sat on a throne wearing shiny silk clothes, her face heavy with makeup. There was an endless line of visitors, gifts and a grand feast.

The ceremony signifies the end of the carefree days of childhood. The girl, now a woman, is ripe for marriage. She needs to cover her bosom, be careful and guard her virtue. She discovers shame and she will carry it for the rest of her life.

The Apsara energy is universally acknowledged as dangerous. The apsaras in mythology were known to seduce the most austere sages from their spiritual pursuits. Most cultures seek to curb and suppress the expression of a young girl's sexuality. The easiest way is to normalize shame around a girl's body by insisting it must be kept hidden and by forbidding any sexual exploration. The other way is to create taboos around anything related to the female body and its functions.

In most parts of India, women are sequestered during the period of menstruation. My grandmother would insist that my sister and I stayed in a separate room during this time—social outcasts who could not contaminate others with their presence or touch. Women do this to themselves in the name of tradition and culture. Rest and recuperation were probably good ideas in the days when women undertook much more manual labour even in the house, but not today. However, menstruation carries the stigma of impurity and being unclean even today. Women are still barred from certain temples to prevent 'pollution' of the sacred space.

Another way to tackle any unwarranted expression of sexual energy was to marry the girl off as soon as possible. Even though it is illegal in India for girls below the age of eighteen to be married, the practice is still prevalent in many parts of the country. According to the organization Girls Not Brides, more than a quarter of Indian girls are married by the age of eighteen. We don't take chances, the Apsara energy can exist safely only within the confines of a marriage.

Apsara's Cultural Coding

As mentioned above, the apsaras of mythology were celestial dancers in Indra's court. They were beautiful, talented and immortal. Some of them were married to the 'gandharvas', the court musicians, but most other apsaras remained single, existing only for the pleasure of the denizens of heaven. The apsaras were deployed by the gods when they wanted to defeat their enemies the asuras, or subdue the saints who could become more powerful than them. Tilottama, an apsara, was created to sow discontent between two powerful and inseparable asura brothers Sunda and Upasunda. Though the brothers shared everything, they beat each other to death while fighting to possess Tilottama. She was duly rewarded for her services with the boon of being able to wander freely across the universe.

Another famous apsara was Menaka. She was sent by Indra to seduce the great sage Vishwamitra, whose austerities were becoming a threat to the power of the gods. Poor Menaka was terrified—sages were known to curse people and mete out cruel and unusual punishments to those who crossed their path—but she had no choice. She danced and sang using all her formidable talents, she transformed the forest to a lush garden, she placed a fragrant garland around his neck but Vishwamitra remained unmoved. The wind god Vayu decided to do his thing and whipped off Menaka's clothes, leaving a naked, beautiful apsara in all her glory. The sage opened his eyes and was smitten. He abandoned his austerities and yielded to bodily pleasures.

In some versions of the story, Menaka and Vishwamitra fall in love with each other. Nevertheless, Vishwamitra is said to have eventually been so angry with Indra, Menaka and himself that he cursed Menaka to be separated from him forever and resumed his austerities. A daughter was born out of this union, but Menaka, being an apsara, could not enjoy the joys of motherhood. She left the baby with a kind sage and went back to heaven. This episode did not end well for her. In some versions of the story, she is reunited with her daughter, Shakuntala; in others, she never meets her. Either way, the pains and pleasures of family life were not for Menaka.

Urvashi, another gorgeous apsara, was supposed to be the most beautiful woman on heaven and earth. She was created by two sages in response to Indra's attempts to tempt them with other beautiful apsaras. The sages Nara and Narayana gifted Urvashi to Indra and she was whisked off to heaven to entertain the gods. Urvashi, on a visit to earth, fell in love with a mortal king called Pururavas. As an apsara, it was impossible for her to marry a mortal. A distracted Urvashi uttered his name in the middle of a dance performance after she returned to heaven, and she was cursed by her irritated dance teacher. He said she would be able to be with the man who occupied her thoughts, but would not be able to live with him if she had a child. So Urvashi did find Pururavas who was pining for her, they did manage to live for a few years together but she was tricked thereafter into returning to heaven by the gods. They missed her too much to allow her some mortal happiness.

An earlier Vedic version states that Urvashi got bored of married life and wanted to return to her female companions and life as a dancer. She had no interest in being a mother and preferred to be a free spirit. This version was successfully overwritten with the more acceptable narrative, mentioned above.

There are many variations of the story of Shoorpanakha, the sister of Ravan, in the Ramayan. She was a beautiful woman but has been depicted as an ugly demoness who faked her appearance to attract men. One fact is consistent. She expressed a desire for Rama but she was ridiculed and had her nose chopped off by Lakshman for her forward behaviour. It was just not done to go after a man, even in the days of yore when men had multiple wives and lovers.

By the seventh century CE or so, we learn of a group of 'servants of god' called the 'devadasis'. These women were talented, skilled dancers attached to local temples. They were free to choose their partners, were economically independent and were respected by the community. Muddupalani (c.1730–1790), a courtesan, poet and dancer, was a jewel in the court of Pratapasimha (c.1739–63), a patron of the arts. She is the author of arguably the first erotic book written by an Indian woman—*Radhika Santawanam*. In a verse, Muddupalani says of herself—'A face that glows like the full moon, skills of conversation matching the countenance, eyes full of compassion matching the speech.' This was an Apsara in her full glory. As time passed, the respect dwindled under the stern gaze of patriarchy. Soon the devadasis were seen as prostitutes, relegated to the fringes of society and found neither respect nor respite from sex slavery. Young girls were forced to become devadasis to support their families. In 1911, almost a century later, an unabridged version of *Radhika Santawanam*, published by another courtesan, Bangalore's Nagaratamma, was banned in India.

The message is clear. There are two kinds of women—the beauteous entertainer and the chaste wife and mother—and never shall the twain meet. Any woman who tries to cross boundaries is doomed. The modern-day Apsara can never hope for a 'normal' mundane existence with a family and the associated social status. She must sing and dance to entertain gods and men. She has a certain kind of freedom, the kind Tilottama received in return for her services.

Films like *Pakeezah* (The Pure One; 1972) and *Umrao Jaan* (1981) tell the stories of Apsaras—beautiful courtesans who cannot find love and a family. The courtesan Sahibjaan was renamed Pakeezah by her lover who wanted to marry her, but she chose to go back to the kotha where she lived rather than tarnish his reputation. Umrao Jaan was kidnapped as a young girl and sold to a brothel. Later she was abandoned by her high-status lover and rejected by her birth family when she finally found her way back to them.

Silk Smitha, the South Indian actress, on whose life the movie *Dirty Picture* (2011) was based, was once the most celebrated 'vamp' in Indian cinema. A song pictured on Silk Smitha in any movie guaranteed a box office hit. At the height of her powers, Silk was a formidable talent. She was naturally sexy, provocative with an earthy appeal that attracted all types of men. Unfortunately, she never found love or respect in her relationships. Silk Smitha committed suicide when she was just thirty-two.

However, even within the socially-sanctioned institution of marriage, the sexual energy of the housewife and mother still needs to be curtailed. Sex is acceptable as long as it is for procreation and with a man. The Urdu writer Ismat Chugtai was charged with obscenity for her short story *Lihaf* (*Quilt*), published in 1942 (Chughtai, 2011).

The story is about Begum Jan, the neglected wife of a Nawab, who is able to find sexual pleasure through a relationship with her female companion, Rabbu. Despite being sequestered in the zenana, she finds her freedom under the forgiving shelter of the quilt. Several years later, film-maker Deepa Mehta made the film *Fire* (1996). Two sisters-in-law, Radha and Sita, are trapped in unhappy marriages. They have no emotional or physical connection with their husbands. It is not unusual for women to stifle their sexuality and sublimate their desires for the sake of family honour and security. But Radha and Sita find love, compassion and an expression of their desires in each other. The film evoked protests from men and women across the country.

In another contemporary film, *Lipstick under My Burkha* (2016), Buaji (aunt; father's sister) is a single older woman, long bereft of companionship. She finds some pleasure in reading erotic novels. However, the act is shameful and has to be done in secret. Society does not acknowledge or allow the physical needs of a single woman to be expressed or fulfilled, especially if she is of a 'certain age'. In fact her identity, even her own name Usha, is erased by the world—she is only Buaji. She develops a crush on a young swimming instructor and seduces him over the phone by pretending to be someone else. All hell breaks loose when the man and the family come to know the truth. Buaji is unceremoniously thrown out of the house. There is no room for the Apsara here. She should have died a long time ago.

Many women have disowned their Apsara because of social conditioning and cultural pressure. In the critically acclaimed film *Masaan* (Crematorium; 2015), Devi Pathak, a young girl in Benares, has illicit sex with a friend, Piyush, in a seedy hotel. She is not queasy or coy about expressing her desire for him or her need for physical intimacy. Devi sneaks into a hotel with her lover, because she cannot openly experiment with her sexuality. She is curious and open as a lover, leading the man in the sexual dance. Devi and Piyush are interrupted by a police raid at the hotel and the policeman takes a photo of her and the boy and blackmails them for 'immoral' behaviour.

Piyush cannot bear the humiliation and commits suicide. Devi stoically continues with her life, even as her father struggles to pay the blackmail money to the policeman. He is surprised not by her action, but by her lack of remorse at behaving like a 'whore'. At work, a colleague misbehaves with her after the incident and when Devi defiantly confronts him, he asks her 'Sharam nahi ati?' (Aren't you ashamed?), implying that her ability to stand and face the world after being exposed is more of a crime than being caught in the act of illicit sex. 'There were two people involved in the act,' retorts Devi as she storms off. It is Devi's ability to transcend shame that is remarkable in a world where women are expected to hide their face and hang their head at the slightest hint of dishonour.

The Apsara archetype still continues to exist beneath the façade of conformity and some women find a safe and acceptable way to channelize their sexual energies. Women like painter Amrita Sher-Gil, actress Parveen Babi and photographer Pamela Bordes blaze briefly in the sky and then, often, are not heard of again. These woman continue to fascinate, inspire, confound and dazzle the rest of the population. There are few true Apsaras that we know about, who are in the public domain.

Apsara's Relationships

The Apsara is very aware of the opposite sex and wants admiration and attention. It is very natural for the young Apsara to want male attention. She is not looking for a serious meaningful relationship. The courting and the dance of attraction appeals to her more than a lasting relationship. She can have many boyfriends, sequentially or simultaneously. She does not think of it as 'cheating'. She has not made any commitment for everlasting love or eternal fidelity. She will be fully present and generous, passionate and fun-loving in a relationship as long as it lasts.

The young Apsara is not ready to be tied down. She knows that the ordinary simple joys of being a wife and managing a home will bore her after a while. She will move from one relationship to another. Many Apsaras will have unhappy marriages. Many will get divorced, believing that they need their freedom to find the 'right one'. Like their mythological counterparts, true Apsaras may never be fully at ease within conventional family life unless they can evoke their Rani energy. Many of them may play the role of a good wife, but they are bored and restless waiting for something more exciting.

The Apsara sees men as a way of fully experiencing her beauty and sensuality. Men are instruments of her expression. She can use them as an artist uses a paintbrush and colours to bring alive a blank canvas. An Apsara in her full power has a seductive pull over men. This kind of power can be heady, potent and often addictive. This is what the Apsara does not want to lose.

Men will be attracted to the Apsara, but they may not necessarily see her as a long-term partner. There is something unattainable about her. A lot of men don't know what to make of her. Her sexuality can be fascinating but intimidating. But the Apsara could also be exploited by an unscrupulous partner to further his own needs, which is why it is imperative for her to remain in charge of her life.

Chetna (Awareness; 1970), a forgotten classic, is about Seema, an unapologetic prostitute, and was a movie way ahead of its time. Here, the heroine has no tragic back-story. She is a true Apsara, in touch with her sexual needs and not squeamish about expressing them. She even falls in love with a nice, kind man and wants to marry him. But her past catches up with them and she gives up her life rather than bring dishonour to her lover.

Some Apsaras dream of a great and magnificent love, much as the Kanya does. No one but a god will satisfy such Apsaras. While the Kanya may compromise and reconcile with the ordinary man, the Apsara keeps searching. If the Apsara has access to her Rani, she will happily settle down with a partner and allow her Apsara to play within the boundaries of a monogamous relationship.

Apsara's Career Choices

Apsaras are natural artists. They usually have a strong sense of aesthetics. Many Apsaras are actresses—the prospect of becoming someone else for a short period appeals to them. Others are painters, poets, sculptors or musicians. They have a flair for design, colour and creativity. They make great dress designers and interior decorators. There is a certain flamboyance in the way they approach their work. Apsaras can be intense and passionate in pursuing their interests, wanting to give their all to their art. They believe in burning brightly even if it is only for a short while.

Apsaras do not thrive in environments that require solitary or routine work, but excel in non-structured environments that involve variety and provide social interactions. They can be entertaining, charming and excel as hostesses and at roles that involve influencing and persuasion. Tilottama, the Apsara, received the gift of being able to go anywhere freely in the universe—this is what every true Apsara wants. A job that takes her to many places and allows exploration of new experiences. The Apsaras do well in the tourism industry as tour guides, travel planners or travel writers. They would love to be in the spotlight and have their own travel show.

They are also great at brokering deals and liaison work that involves bringing people together, and make great lobbyists. They prefer the nebulous to the concrete and one of their strengths is managing ambiguity. They also work well as independent service providers and freelancers, leaving the paperwork and structuring to others and move on to the next challenge.

If Apsaras integrate the powers of the Rani or Veera, they can become determined and focused and excel in their career. Without that, they may flit from one job to another, looking for the right thing.

Apsara as a Leader

Apsaras become leaders by excelling in their chosen fields. Though driven by passion and purpose, they lack patience and rigour to build organizations and systems and need others to help them do so. They make for charming and popular leaders, who channelize their seductive energy to influence others and get them to do the work. They cultivate their own brand image well and are good networkers. They know how to handle men and an intelligent Apsara will use her powers well to align with them. Sometimes, this may alienate women colleagues, but this is a price the Apsara leader is willing to pay.

Apsaras often face the 'double bind' bias at work—a woman cannot be both beautiful and smart! An article in the *Harvard Business Review* (Wieckowski, 2019) discusses research findings by professors Leah Sheppard (Washington State University) and Stefanie Johnson (University of Colorado Boulder)—beautiful women are perceived to be less truthful, less worthy as leaders and more deserving of termination. They pay the 'beauty penalty'. Less attractive women are seen as more honest and trustworthy than both attractive men and women. The research found no difference in perception of men based on their attractiveness.

Many Apsara women in leadership roles tone down their beauty so that they will be taken seriously. Apsaras who are secure in their power will create their own style, but cultivate other behaviours which will build trust and create connections. Ideally, an Apsara leader needs to get a good solid team behind her, including a personal assistant who will take care of the daily routine and allow her to soar and dream big. She needs to nurture this team and focus on their needs to ensure her success.

AMRITA SHER-GIL: THE APSARA WHO LOVED SEX AND ART

Amrita Sher-Gil died in 1941 at the age of twenty-eight, but she lived lifetimes in those years. She is one of India's foremost artists and one of her paintings sold for Rs 18.6 crore in 2018 at an auction by Sotheby's. A road in Delhi has been named after her, and the Government of India has declared her works as national art treasures. She is recognized as a leader and pioneer in the world of Indian art.

Her paintings are known for their rich, deep colours, and her life was just as colourful. Amrita was in touch with her body and unashamed about her need for love and sex. She painted herself naked from the waist up in a painting called 'Self Portrait as a Tahitian', an ode to Gauguin. She experimented with the female form in many of her paintings of nude women, exploring the sexuality and identity of women in most of her paintings.

As an artist, Amrita truly came into her own when she moved back to India from Paris, claiming the country as her own. She wrote, 'I realized my artistic mission then: to interpret the life of Indians and particularly of the poor Indians pictorially, to paint those silent images of infinite submission and patience, to depict their angular brown bodies' (Archer, 1959). She was drawn to painting women and depicted them with a keen empathy that male painters did not have. 'Amrita herself seems to have felt inclined toward a lesbian encounter, partly as a result of her larger view of woman as a strong individual liberated from the artifice of convention,' says her biographer Yashodhara Dalmia (Dalmia, 2006). Amrita also travelled widely, unusual for a woman in her times. Hungary, India, France and back to India, where she moved between Simla, Uttar Pradesh and Lahore.

She had a varied and tempestuous love-life. At the age of sixteen, she went to live in Paris with her mother, a Hungarian opera singer. There she is alleged to have had a homosexual affair with her room-mate, Marie Louise, and later an affair with painter Boris Taslitzky while studying. She later became engaged to a rich Indian landowner, Yusuf Khan, but he was forbidden by his family from marrying her. She had a brief affair with a British journalist, Malcolm Muggeridge. She later married Victor Egan, a cousin from her mother's side and is said, to have had affairs with men and women throughout her married life.

She is also said to have attracted the attention of Jawaharlal Nehru, who admired her art. The two exchanged several letters, which were later burnt by Amrita's parents. Amrita was once invited to attend a party by the renowned journalist Khushwant Singh. She is said to have called his son 'an ugly child', which enraged Mrs Singh, who promptly knocked her off the guest list. Amrita vowed to take revenge by seducing Khushwant Singh, which, according to him, she sadly never did.

Amrita did not censure her life or art. Rumours still have it that her early and unnatural death was due to either a botched abortion or poisoning by her husband who had grown tired of her numerous affairs. Whatever the truth, there can be no doubt that Amrita lived fully, explosively, and had a vast appetite for the world and its experiences.

Apsara's Power Sources: Self-Expression and the Power to Influence

The Apsara in her full power is a breathtaking force of nature. She may not be conventionally pretty, but has a certain energy and presence that cannot be ignored. Men and women are drawn into her orbit and she holds court with aplomb. She derives her power from her ability to be influential and to express herself freely. The Apsara is the only female power archetype able to acknowledge and channelize her sexual energy. This helps her to be creative and innovative in ways others cannot imagine. She is a wild woman, untrammelled by conventions and artifice.

The Apsara does not worry about what people will say about her. She is able to subordinate her need for acceptance to her desire for freedom. Her fearlessness in this regard allows her to be her authentic self. She inspires other women to shed their inhibitions and express themselves. The Apsara shows us who we can be: gorgeous, free, wild creatures of the universe.

Apsara's Core Need: Self-Expression

The Apsara wants to be loved and desired but these are subordinate to her deepest need for full self-expression. This starts with her own self, and her body. The body is the Apsara's first canvas. She adorns it, she cares for it and uses it well. She likes an audience. Like her celestial counterparts, she wants the world as her stage. This aspect—being seen and acknowledged by others—energizes her, it feeds her own desire. She will perform for others, use others, often be used by others but they will never know her true soul.

The Apsara is creative and her best creation is her own self. This creation needs to be exhibited and shown to the world. The Apsara's need for validation is different from the Kanya's. While the Kanya needs acceptance from others and acknowledgement of her goodness, the Apsara wants to be adored and even worshipped.

Apsara's Power Blocks

The Apsara, more than any other archetype, is prone to excesses. Her power is blocked by an abundance of an energy that she cannot channel in a constructive way. If she is unable to invoke other powers, the Apsara's self-sabotaging behaviour can become a danger to herself and others.

Emotionally Drained by: Melancholy and Mania

The real world is too mundane and can never match up to the heaven that the Apsara dreams of. Even as she tries hard to be rooted to the earth, she longs for her own celestial abode. The men she meets never seem to live up to her expectations. Her energy and enthusiasm flare and dissipate as her passion can never find fulfilment. In most archetypal studies, the dark side of the lover is the prostitute who sells her soul and loses her sense of self-worth.

At this stage, some Apsaras seek solace in alcohol and promiscuity and begin a spiral of self-destruction. The world does not offer them what they want so they turn their back on it. Unable to channel their power, they lose themselves in a haze of melancholy, drowning in the sadness of unfulfilled expectations.

An Apsara unable to find a steady partner, who can give her space and help her rein-in her energy, can become a problem for herself and others. In a patriarchal society, such 'wayward women' are often seen as crazy or wild. Many repent and reconcile to their fate; some commit suicide.

Patriarchy makes adulterous women face consequences, not men. They are stoned, raped, burnt and killed. Anna Karenina, Madame Bovary and Maya Memsahib have to die to pay for their transgressions. Some, like Marilyn Monroe, Madhubala, Silk Smitha, Amrita Sher-Gil, flare into prominence like a comet and then vanish, almost as though they were called away to heaven; the earth could not hold them.

Real-life Apsaras are not immortal and when they disappear, they leave behind broken hearts and broken homes.

Fears: Suppression

The Apsara's biggest fear is the loss of her precious freedom. She worries that she will be stifled and smothered by those who do not understand her. She longs for freedom that allows her unrestrained expression. She laughs wildly, loves madly, dances with abandon and hates intensely. Her gypsy soul does not want to be tied down.

Yet, the world is not often kind to Apsaras. It demands that they give freely of their beauty and art, but it does not give them the freedom of choice and agency that they crave, in return. The Apsara is thus the beautiful song bird who must be locked up in a cage so that she does not fly away—and this is what the Apsara fears the most. So she preens her feathers and sings her sweetest song hoping to be rewarded with love and freedom. Yet, the more accomplished she becomes and the more she shines, the greater the chance of her being confined. The bars of the gilded cage only grow stronger and harder.

Anarkali, the dancer in the court of Emperor Akbar, was the most beautiful and accomplished performer of her time. Yet, the more mesmerizingly she danced, the greater grew the danger to her freedom. Prince Salim became besotted by her beauty and charm. Since no courtesan could marry a royal prince, Anarkali was doomed to a tragic end. In the classic movie *Mughal-e-Azam* (The Great Mughal; 1960), Anarkali (played by Madhubala) dares the great Mughal emperor with a song: 'Pyar kiya to darna kya/Pyar kiya, koi chori nahi ki/ Ghut ghut aahe bharna kya' (What's to fear in love/I've loved, not stolen/ Why should I suffer in silence?). The emperor did not take kindly to it. He had her sealed into a wall. The only freedom left to her was to die in that airless prison. This is the actual nightmare of all Apsaras.

Responds with: Manipulation and Deception

The Apsara wants to be centre-stage, beloved of the gods. She is prone to jealousy and insecurity. She believes that in order to gain freedom and power, she must placate those who hold power. Despite having great personal charm and power, she worries that others may be more beautiful and accomplished and may get a greater share of the adoration.

This makes her manipulative and deceptive—she uses her charms and wiles to win over those in power so that her wishes will be granted. And this is why other women do not like or trust Apsaras. The wives of powerful men are especially wary of Apsaras. 'Here comes the heartbreaker and homewrecker,' they feel. The Apsara is the manic 'other woman', who will stop at nothing to get the man.

In pursuit of her own ends, the Apsara can lose sight of her responsibilities; her appetites and desires appear to be insatiable and extravagant in the world of conventions. Sometimes, she suppresses her Apsara energy in the interest of survival and sometimes she is able to gracefully channel it and embrace other roles in her life. Sometimes, she is unable to find a way to lead a wholesome life.

The Apsara's power is diminished by a melancholic streak and by her irresponsible and manipulative behaviour. She is most prone to self-sabotage among all the six power archetypes and in the end, becomes her worst enemy.

How the Apsara Grows

Eat, Pray, Love by Elizabeth Gilbert became a publishing phenomenon, selling millions of copies, befuddling even the author (Gilbert, 2007). The book begins with Liz on the bathroom floor, hopeless, depressed, at her lowest point and ends with her finding love and peace across three countries.

There is no story more compelling than this on the redemption of the degraded Apsara. I recently had the opportunity to attend a book reading by Elizabeth Gilbert in Gurugram, where I live. I was charmed and moved by the candid conversation and her powerful yet gracious presence. Here was a woman who had been through some serious stuff and not just survived, but grown. This was a far cry from the self-confessed seduction addict, the rootless flaky Apsara. Elizabeth Gilbert seemed more like a wise Rishika without a Rishika's arrogance and disconnection, but one who retained the charm of an Apsara. She seemed like a woman who had found her true self, embraced that self with love and was now free to love not just herself but the whole world.

The Apsara grows by finding her feet on earth. She needs a strong grounding energy to save herself from falling prey to melancholy. The grounding energy can come with stillness and self-reflection. Often, it is through love. Actress and former Miss Universe Sushmita Sen is an Apsara with strong Veera powers as well, who has grown into wholeness without losing herself. She bucked convention by adopting two daughters, and brings them up as a single mother, fully invoking her Ma energies. She speaks her mind and buys her own diamonds instead of expecting a man to give them to her. She has had many men in her life. In an interview on Simi Garewal's talk show, she stated that she saw these lovers as catalysts for her own growth and expression. She remains unmarried.

Sushmita Sen has found a deep grounding energy in her love for her two daughters, for whom she provides a secure and stable environment. She has a loving connection to her body and her beauty. She is not a prolific actress or a model now, but is still a role model for many young women. Her unconventional life is seen as an example of women's empowerment.

The Hindi movie *Fashion* (2008) is set in the modelling world, favoured by many Apsaras. The heroine, Meghna Mathur, starts off as a shy Kanya who is hesitant to model lingerie and is squeamish about exposing her body. However, she is able to soon invoke her Apsara to serve her ambitious Veera, and becomes the top model in India. She becomes more comfortable with her body and grows in confidence. On the way to the top, she seduces her rich sponsor, alienates other women and falls into a vortex of excesses—drinks, drugs and dumb boyfriends. Her Apsara energy tips over to the shadow side. She needs to return to her childhood home, reclaim her lost Kanya, accept her mistakes and redeem herself through kindness and humility. Another Apsara character, Shonali Gujral, a model and ex-prima donna, unfortunately succumbs to her excesses and dies of a drug overdose. In attempting to save Shonali, Meghna saves and steadies herself.

The Apsara does not have to fall to the bathroom floor or go into rehab or a retreat to grow. She needs to recognize and accept her Apsara nature without guilt or shame. She can then channel her abundant energy into a passion and purpose. She needs to identify her shadow power, often the Rani or Rishika energies which she has not acknowledged earlier.

A smart Apsara will surround herself with wise friends who can hold her energy and give her space. She will not hesitate to ask for help if she finds herself in a hole. Many Apsaras need women friends and nurturing family members to support them. She has to summon the courage to ask for forgiveness and humility to accept her mistakes, since she may have alienated many of the people around her.

The Apsara needs to strengthen her connection to the earth. She needs to slow down and put roots. She needs to understand that with freedom comes great responsibility. Once the Apsara is able to hold both with ease, she can shine in her full glorious power and illuminate those around her.

Case Studies

Mitali

Mitali is an acquaintance I bump into from time to time at get-togethers. When I first met her seven years ago, Mitali was a very attractive, married woman with two lovely children and an adoring husband. She seemed to be a happy homemaker who dabbled in art during her 'spare time'. She had a wonderful sense of style. All the women appreciated the way she put herself together and all the men were drawn to her seductive energy.

When I met Mitali after a few months, I came to know that she was in the middle of a messy divorce. Her husband had discovered her secret affair with a neighbour. Mitali confessed that she had felt stifled in her marriage and had lost the connection with her husband. She had embarked on the affair without much thought, to 'fill the gaping hole in my love life'. She had dreams and desires, all of which had been suppressed within the confines of marriage and motherhood.

After three years of an ugly legal battle, she got joint custody of her children. Mitali grew up and grew wiser through this tough time. She found an anchor in yoga and started teaching art to underprivileged children. Mitali, the Apsara, seemed to come alive after her divorce. She found new strength and a new passion. She faced down the accusing stares and ignored the gossip. She adapted to the single life easily and began to take time out for her art. I see her invoking the Rishika and Ma energies actively. Mitali is still an Apsara who is on a journey of self-discovery and acceptance.

Noor

Noor, a client-servicing manager in an advertising agency, quit her job in a huff. An attractive woman who dressed well and laughed with gusto, Noor had got along very well with the creative team at work and had been valued for her abilities to build great relationships with clients. But she felt that her manager, a woman, was 'against her' from the very beginning.

She believed that this boss sabotaged her career and refused to let her grow. 'Women are each other's worst enemies', said Noor. She got along much better with men than with women. The young male brand managers in the client organization 'ate out of her hands', but the women thwarted her ambitions and did not like her.

Noor, the Apsara, was unable to see her women colleagues as anything but competitors. Her insecurity made her suspicious and alienated her from the other women in her team. She did not share information with them and spoke to them only when she wanted something.

The women she worked with felt that she was manipulative and used her looks to get ahead. Noor was not aware of how other women experienced her and finally quit her job in a huff, blaming her manager. In her next job at a small firm founded by one of her former company's clients, she was more comfortable. She had a male boss and felt that she could handle him well. She stayed in that role for a couple of years, but was unable to make it to the next level. She quit again, blaming it on the wife of the boss who 'hated her guts', and the boss who had let her down.

Thereafter, unable to find a suitable role in any agency or organization, Noor decided to start her own public relations consultancy. She was talented and had good networking skills. Soon, Noor had a few commissions from small brands for media-consultancy projects. She had a couple of boyfriends, and was facing pressure from her parents to get married. However, Noor had not yet found a man she could really care for, nor was the business doing as well as she thought it would. So she agreed to marry the rich businessman her family had chosen for her.

The man was ten years older than Noor. He had a very different temperament and very different thinking . Though Noor could not connect to her husband initially, she found him to be steady and loyal. To her surprise, she found that her husband gave her the freedom, independence and assurance that she needed. He supported her business and referred clients to her PR firm. With his support, she became more calm, steady and understanding. They went on to have a relationship of mutual respect and trust.

6

Veera: The Rebel Warrior

Subhadra Kumari Chauhan's famous poem *Jhansi ki Rani* has these immortal lines, 'Bundele, harbolo ke muh, hamne suni kahani thi/Khoob ladi mardani, who toh Jhansi wali Rani thi.' (We heard this from the Bundelas themselves/That she fought as valiantly as a man, after all she was the Rani of Jhansi.)

All cultures speak of the warrior energy in women—Athena, the goddess of war, Diana the huntress, Durga the vanquisher of demons. The Veera embodies the energy of action and resolution. A Veera is bold, unafraid as she ventures out into the unknown. She is a problem-solver, a leader and a director of enterprises. She is often a restless soul, who does not like to sit still for a minute. She is forever busy, running from one task to another making sure each one is executed flawlessly.

She usually does not care for the opinion of others and can be headstrong and reckless. The mature Veera is aware of her power and uses it well, usually in service of a cause. She is angered by injustice and will fight valiantly for a just cause. She is relentless in pursuit of her goals. She perseveres and sticks it out longer than most others, overcoming the hurdles in her path through tenacity and grit.

As a young girl, the Veera is a problem child for parents. She is the 'tomboy' who prefers to play rough games with the boys. She does not listen to her parents. She is a rule breaker; the opposite of the Kanya who prefers compliance to conflict. The Veera is seen as irresponsible and rebellious and is often punished for this rebellious streak. She doesn't care.

If the punishment is severe and consistent, her Veera spirit may be contained. She will become a tamed Veera, who is either outwardly obedient while seething inside and sneaking out to break rules, or a subdued Veera who 'for her own good' seeks to adopt the behaviours of a good girl.

Many girls become Veeras as a replacement for the boy their parents never had. They are treated by the parents as the 'son' of the family and learn to behave like one, eschewing feminine trappings for short hair and boyish clothes. The blockbuster film *Dangal* (Wrestling Bout; 2016) is based on a true story. Wrestler Mahendra Phogat—though initially disappointed at not having sons—trained his daughters, Gita and Babita, to become champion wrestlers. The movie shows the girls cutting off their long hair, throwing off their dupattas and getting down to the wrestling mat with gusto. If Mahendra Phogat had sons to fulfil his dreams, the girls would have been like any other girl in rural Haryana—married-off by eighteen and managing a brood of children in their twenties.

A Veera who has loving parents as a child and receives proper guidance grows into a mature adolescent who is brave and self-willed. She is able to exert her power without offending others and without being a rebel. She takes constructive action instead of reacting on impulse. The young

Veera is able to exert her agency and make decisions about her future. She will embark on an adventure, ready to take risks and accept the consequences.

Since the expression of the Veera energy in women has rarely been encouraged by tradition or religion, this energy has been suppressed in many Indian women. Temper tantrums by little boys are tolerated but little girls are told to shut up and put up. Most decisions are made for women by men. Dependence and submission have been the norm. The Veera's independence, self-reliance and assertion of her own rights is seen as 'unfeminine' and dangerous.

The Veera power is the one most aligned to the masculine. Several Veeras emulate men they admire and attempt to 'be like a man' to gain legitimacy and respect. Sometimes, this behaviour goes against them and they end up alienating both men and women.

Veera's Cultural Coding

The demon Mahishasur had received a divine boon that he could not be killed by any man. Obviously, there was no woman who could kill him either. So the divine trinity of Shiva, Vishnu and Brahma created Durga. She emerged fully formed, like Athena who sprang fully formed out of Zeus's head. Durga was a female manifestation of the male warrior energy. She was fearsome, arrogant, brave and indomitable. She easily defeated and killed the evil demon. Durga is still worshipped all across India. The Durga pooja in East India is the main festival of the region, where the goddess, in all her glory, is worshipped over ten days.

The eight-armed goddess is always depicted with a foot on the body of the vanquished demon. Durga, Kali, Chandi—the fierce goddess is known by many names and is seen as a symbol of woman power, but she remains a male creation always aligned to the male gods. Thus the warrior energy has always been associated with men. Women were forbidden to fight in the armies and it was against the 'dharma' of a man to fight with a woman.

This is best illustrated by the story of Amba in the Mahabharat. She was the eldest daughter of the king of Kashi, and was in love with the prince of Shalva. Bhishma came to her swayamvar, abducted her and her two sisters and presented all three to Vichitravirya, the king of the Kurus, as his brides. Amba's sisters agreed to be his queens, but Amba told Vichitravirya about her love for the prince of Shalva. Vichitravirya honourably sent her off to the prince, who refused to accept her since she had been carried away by another man.

When Amba returned, Vichitravirya refused to take her back since she had been cast away by another man. So Amba turned to Bhishma, the man who was responsible for this entire mess. He cited his vow of celibacy and refused to accept her as his wife. Having been kicked to and fro like a football, Amba was enraged and humiliated. She wanted revenge and prayed to Lord Shiva, 'I am a weak woman. How can I defeat a great warrior like Bhishma?'

She was told she would be able to do it in her next life when she would be reborn as a man. So Amba jumped into fire, died and was reborn as Shikandi, the son of King Drupad. In some versions of this story, Shikandi is described as a transgendered person, born a woman who became a man. In any case, Amba had to become Shikandi to fight against Bhishma.

Faced by Shikhandi on the battlefield of Kurukshetra, and knowing that Shikandi was born a woman, Bhishma refused to fight. Shikandi duly shot Bhishma full of arrows and marked the beginning of the end of the great battle.

This story, to me, speaks of the powerlessness of the angry woman who had to become a man to take revenge.

Draupadi, another strong woman with the fiery Veera energy, had to bear the ignominy of being shared by five brothers. She paid the price for a reckless remark about Duryodhan with public disrobement. Her five husbands were powerless to protect her—the woman was a community property that they had gambled away. Later, while in exile, Draupadi had to ward off the attention of Keechak, a commander in King Virat's army. Her husband, Bhim, had to step in and kill Keechak to teach him a lesson. Even a great and powerful queen had to depend on a man to save her honour. Draupadi had to wait many years for her husbands to fight in the great war to finally get her revenge against Duryodhan.

Kaikeyi, one of the wives of King Dashrath in the Ramayan, has been branded as the 'wicked' queen who sent beloved Rama into exile. But she had not always been an insecure, vindictive woman. A skilled charioteer, she had gone into battle with her husband, and then saved his life after he was injured on the battlefield. The grateful king granted her two boons of her choosing, and she took a promise from him that she could ask for these at a time of her choosing. Known for her short temper, she nevertheless was the king's favourite wife and the other more submissive queens were jealous and envious of her ability to hold her own.

Such a woman could not always have her own way. In the epic, we find a maid called Manthara who fills Kaikeyi's ears, telling her that Rama is the favoured son and Bharat, Kaikeyi's son, will get nothing. Over time, Kaikeyi is influenced enough to ask for Rama's exile as one her boons. Later she is shown to bitterly repent this lapse in judgement and begs forgiveness from Rama after his return. But, to date, she is known only as the evil queen, the villainess of the Ramayan.

South India celebrates the festival of Deepavali to commemorate the triumph of good over evil, in this case, the killing of the demon Narakasura by Lord Krishna. I did not know, until recently, that Narakasura was actually killed by Krishna's wife, the warrior queen Satyabhama. Both Krishna and Satyabhama set out to kill the demon as equal partners, and it was Satyabhama who drew her bow and killed him.

What we remember of Satyabhama is her arrogance, haughtiness, possessiveness and the stories that teach her a lesson. Satyabhama was jealous of Rukmini, Krishna's chief queen, who seems like a mature sedate Rani. When Krishna presented Rukmini with beautiful parijata flowers, Satyabhama wanted them too. She demanded the whole tree, which was duly planted in her garden, adjacent to Rukmini's garden. But when the tree burst into flower, the blossoms fell on Rukmini's side, causing Satyabhama much grief.

In another story, Satyabhama wanted to show her love for the lord and win his favour. Egged on by Narada, she decided to weigh Krishna against every precious thing she had. She placed Krishna on one side of a giant weighing scale and all her jewels and ornaments on the other. But the scales wouldn't budge. Everything was removed. Then Rukmini placed a single tulsi leaf on it and the scale on which Krishna sat, rose till both scales were perfectly balance. It is only humility and devotion that pleases the lord. Satyabhama learnt her lesson and ate humble pie.

In our culture, a woman's anger and display of aggression or power is justified only if it is in service of her husband or children. In the story *Silapaddikaram* from Tamil Nadu, Kannagi is the virtuous wife of Kovalan, a merchant. Kovalan is a weak-willed man who falls for the charms of Madhavi, a courtesan he meets in the course of his travels. He abandons Kannagi. But she, the loyal wife, waits for him to return and kindly accepts him despite his affair. Kovalan then falls on hard times. When he goes to sell his wife's anklet in the market, he is wrongly imprisoned and executed on the charge of stealing the queen's anklet. Both anklets look similar.

When Kannagi hears of this, her fury at the injustice done to her husband overtakes her anguish. She storms into the Pandya king's court and flings her other anklet. Hers is filled with pearls while the queen had precious gems in hers. The king realizes his mistake and apologizes, begging for forgiveness. But Kannagi's fury does not abate until she burns the entire kingdom, ridding the land of all evil elements. Now, she is the avenging Veera in her full power. There is a statue of Kannagi on the boulevard at Marina beach, hailing her as one of the heroines of Tamil literature.

There have been several warrior Veera queens in our history, but we have not heard of many of them or celebrated them. For instance, Rani Rudramma Devi of the Kakatiya dynasty became queen in 1263 CE. She was brought up as a boy and dressed like a man, leading her troops in battle. Velu Nachiyar, the eighteenth-century queen from Sivagangai in Tamil Nadu, was the first to resist the colonial ambitions of the British. She successfully forged alliances and fought against them to retrieve her kingdom. Bibi Sahib Kaur, the older sister of the ruler of Patiala, played an active role in the region from 1793–1801 CE. She not only rescued her husband from the rebel forces, but stepped in to run her brother's kingdom after her marriage. Later, Maharani Jind Kaur, the widow of Sikh ruler Ranjit Singh, waged two wars against the British. She was separated from her young son, exiled from her beloved Punjab and cheated by the British but remained resilient and undaunted till the end.

Rani Lakshmibai of Jhansi brings to mind the iconic image of the brave queen on horseback, brandishing a sword, her infant child strapped to her back. We find this statue in many parts of India. Manikarnika was born in 1828 to an ordinary family in Varanasi. She learnt to read and write, and was also taught horsemanship, fencing and archery. The young girl's bravery and valour attracted the attention of the king's minister and Manikarnika was duly married to King Gangadhar Rao. When he died, she rebelled against the British and refused to cede the kingdom. Instead, she went into exile, rallied her troops and made a valiant attempt to win back her kingdom. Though she succumbed to her injuries on the battlefield more than 200 years ago, she still holds sway in our nation's collective consciousness. The movie *Manikarnika* (2019) celebrated this queen who was much ahead of her times.

There are many more Veeras who took charge, fought hard and vanquished their enemies with the full force of their warrior energy. We have forgotten most of them. However, today there are more women who are educated, working, taking on leadership roles and excelling in traditionally masculine sports like boxing and wrestling. Until recently, women could not hold permanent commissions in the

Indian armed forces. A landmark ruling by the Supreme Court in 2020 has now allowed women to get permanent commissions. The apex court said that the Centre's opposition to this perpetuated gender stereotypes, a mindset that needed to change.

Gender stereotypes are changing, but slowly.

Veera's Relationships

The Veera often carries herself like a man. She feels that she is just as strong and does not need a man to take care of her. She is attracted only to someone stronger and more powerful than her, someone who is the Veer to her Veera. She is quick to dismiss most men as weak or spineless. The Veera woman can scare many men off with her independence, anger, recklessness and outspokenness. She calls a spade a spade and welcomes a transparent honest relationship of equals, if not she would rather be alone; Durga and Kali do not have consorts.

She needs a man who can match her resolute energy and can handle her personality, instead of being overpowered by it. The Veera woman respects a man's strength when it is the quiet strength of a confident man, rather than the macho chest-thumping bravado of an immature man. The Veera woman will not pander or pamper her man. So, if a man needs to bask in maternal coziness or find a seductive siren in the bedroom, the Veera is not the woman for him.

In popular literature and cinema, the Veera woman is 'tamed' by the man. Her wildness and wilfulness cannot lead to a peaceful union so she must be 'domesticated', often by force and a show of strength. If she retaliates with a slap, she is made to pay the price just as Draupadi did. After being humiliated, she is expected to come around and permit the advances of the man she spurned. In many parts of our country, a woman who has been raped is 'allowed' to marry her rapist, thus normalizing the use of force against women. Many Veeras have been beaten into submission by their men and they learn to lie quietly like wounded dragons in the ashes of their dreams.

Indian film songs insist that a woman's 'No' is equal to a 'Yes'. In the Hindi film *Josh* (Fervour; 1990), the song insists that 'Hoton pe na, dil mein haan hoenga. Yeh uska style hoenga' (Her lips say no, but her heart says yes. This must be her style). It is inconceivable for a woman to have the audacity to refuse a man's advances. So strong is this trope that it continues to be used in all cultures. The Mills and Boon romances that I read many years ago as a teenager usually featured a sardonic, arrogant hero who savaged the high-spirited heroine, kissing her and touching her without her consent, until she relented in the last few pages.

A mature Veera can tread the fine line between authenticity and diplomacy. She allows her fire to burn but ensures that it will never inflame tensions in a loving relationship.

Veera's Career Choices

The Veera is a natural director and team leader, a good executor who is particular about meeting deadlines. Always a doer, she excels in a role that she feels strongly about. Since she is aggressive and goal-oriented, she can make a great salesperson.

The quick-thinking Veera is often impatient for results and gets easily bored of repetitive tasks that don't challenge her. Needless to say, the Veera does not do well in careers that involve data analysis, or research projects that drag on.

She would rather be up and about, doing things and getting things done.

The Veera is happy to undertake new projects, taking risks if needed. She easily adapts to change and is a good problem-solver. In fact, many Veeras become entrepreneurs and chart their own course. They also thrive in start-ups with few rules and processes, and greater freedom to innovate. Veeras don't mind working hard as long as they are headed towards a goal. Many Veeras who have not found their niche may keep moving from one role or job to another hankering after challenges where she can prove herself, but a Veera who has found her cause or calling will be able to adapt and forge ahead and do whatever it takes to succeed in that role. The outcome-oriented Veera will invoke other energies in the service of her goal.

Veera as a Leader

The Veera believes that she is a born leader. This is the 'bossy' child who gets others to play the games she wants, who loves giving orders and usually gets her way through sheer force of will. The Veera who does not become temperamentally mature as she grows up becomes an immature leader who is a terror. Such Veeras gain power by dominating their team and ordering them around. They do not delegate important tasks, believing that only they are capable of doing them. Command and control is their default mode.

The mature Veera, however, is a confident woman who believes that she can take charge and lead her team. She does not shy away from responsibility, solves the problems of others, welcomes challenges and inspires trust. She loves to achieve and accomplish goals and this makes her a very good leader.

Mature Veeras who are in their power know how to channel their energy. Every woman who has reached a certain position of leadership has to draw on the Veera energies to set and accomplish goals. Even Mother Teresa, who was the epitome of compassion and Ma energy, had a strong Veera core that helped her to grow her charitable organization into a formidable force for good. She would go around Kolkata scolding, begging and influencing the rich to donate to her cause. She worked hard and led a large group of nuns to reduce poverty and provide care for the sick and needy.

THE KALI FROM KALIGHAT, MAMATA BANERJEE: THE VEERA AT WORK

Mamata Banerjee, the chief minister of West Bengal, has been described as mercurial, temperamental and fearless in several articles and biographies. She is the undisputed head of the Trinamool Congress party and is the only woman chief minister in India at this time. 'Didi' or elder sister, as she is called, is one of the few women politicians in India to have made it on her own. She had no political connections or well-placed relations. Didi has never married. Her entire life has been spent in the single-minded achievement of her goals and fulfilling her mission of public service.

She became active in student politics in college and first came to the notice of the Congress Party leaders as a protestor. She went on to establish the students wing of the Congress Party, and she was at the forefront of rallies. Shutapa Paul writes in her book *Didi: The Untold Mamata Banerjee:* 'When he (JP [Jayprakash Narayan]) was in Calcutta to rally the masses against Indira, Mamata blocked his convoy and threw herself on the ground. With this show of bravado, senior Congress leaders were forced to notice the new kid on the block' (Paul, 2018).

Mamata made her way up the ranks through sheer grit, determination and audacity. Like a true Veera, she fought-off contenders from her own party, misogynistic attacks by the opposition and a weary public to win the elections against the Communist Party (Marxist), the CPM, which had been in power in the state for thirty-five years.

Her reign has been controversial. Didi is a strong critic of the ruling government and Prime Minister Modi, and is one of the few people to voice her criticisms so vocally in public. She is not a woman who minces her words. A fiery orator, she strides across the stage, waving her hands vigorously, chastising her opponents and rousing the rabble with poetry and passion. Mamatadi is rather like the 'kal baishakhi', the violent summer thunderstorms that strike her home state every year. They bring relief to the pre-kharif crops, provide respite from the sultry heat, but are also capable of damage and destruction.

In the opinion of another biographer, Dola Mitra, Didi's excessive self-confidence and inability to admit her mistakes is her tragic flaw (Mitra 2014). The author notes that she can be dictatorial, whimsical, short-tempered and arrogant. She has a tendency to shoot-off her mouth without thinking and refuses to acknowledge her mistakes. When she was impatient and upset with the handling of the Amphan cyclone in West Bengal, she angrily told the people to 'chop off her head'. She was also widely criticized for her remarks on the rape cases in West Bengal. Though Didi does not seem to speak with malice, she comes across as thoughtless and insensitive.

If Mamata Banerjee can transcend the scrappy street-fighter aspect of her Veera energy, and move to the mature Veera who is more stable, thoughtful and circumspect, she can become a highly respected leader on the national stage.

Veera's Power Source: The Drive to Win

The Veera derives her power from her ability to take risks, to go after a goal, and to stay focused on the task ahead to secure victory. Like the courageous warrior, she forges ahead, quelling enemies and overcoming obstacles. The Veera is expressing her full power when she is achieving something, when she is on a quest.

She is resolute, competitive, ambitious and does not take 'no' for an answer. Her power lies in her unique gift of relentless pursuit and perseverance. When she combines her fiery energy with her dogged determination, she is a formidable force to reckon with.

Veera's Core Need: Achievement

The Veera has a strong achievement orientation. Accomplishing goals and making things happen give her a sense of self-determination. She derives her self-esteem from her actions and achievements. Her identity is linked to doing rather than being. She feels the need to make her mark and exercise her agency. Action is everything. Passivity is death. The feeling that she has accomplished something difficult gives her a great sense of satisfaction. She thrives in difficult situations where she can be the heroine, win the war and save the day. The journey does not matter to the Veera. The end justifies the means.

The Veera's need for achievement through self-determination shows up as rebellion against authority. Authority might force her to conform, to be like everyone else. The Veera cannot stand that. She believes that she is entitled to her own way, her own opinions, her decisions, and the right to choose her path. The Veera often becomes the champion in other people's quest for self-determination, a cause which she takes on as her own. She is the freedom fighter who can rally others to the cause. She first fights for her own freedom.

Veera's Power Blocks

The Veera's need to achieve can become an obsession. This is her undoing. Her fiery power is doused by her own energy drainers. The Veera in her single-minded quest is unable to see that she is her own enemy.

Emotionally Drained by: Suppressed Rage

Due to cultural conditioning, anger is not seen as a positive emotion for a woman. Anger can be a positive emotion as it propels people to act in the face of atrocity or injustice. The anger over the horrific rape of a young woman on a bus, known as the Nirbhaya case, has led to greater punishment for rapists. Angry women can change the world if they can channel their anger well. But women are taught to suppress and swallow their anger. There is no 'angry young woman' prototype that is held up as a role model. A woman's anger, thus, often festers beneath the surface, leaking out as sarcastic comments, or erupting like a volcano that cannot be controlled.

Many suppressed Veeras carry their rage within them. They feel angry with themselves for compromising with the world, they feel angry with the world for making them adjust to its demands, they feel angry at the injustice of it all.

While anger provides fuel and is useful to protect ourselves against danger, the immature Veera's propensity to anger is often her undoing. She is impatient, easily frustrated and always on the edge. If the Veera does not get her away, she is consumed by rage. She lashes out, wounding others in her way, much like an angry animal. Her survival instincts make her fight rather than opt for flight or freeze in any situation.

The intensity of the Veera's anger is inversely proportional to her sense of self and identity. Veeras who are secure and confident do not anger easily. Insecure Veeras who live with a constant fear of failure are short-tempered. They rave and rant in the moments when they feel threatened and then subside leaving the wreckage of their wrath about them. Rage drains the Veera and leaves her exhausted. When her fury controls her, she becomes out of control.

Fears: Failure

The fear of failure haunts all Veeras and can also block their power. The warrior fears defeat more than anything else. The idealized warrior prefers death to surrender. The desire to avoid failure at all costs makes the Veera an insecure, driven perfectionist. Failure in anything that the Veera sets out to accomplish feels like death. She will do anything to avoid that pain.

Responds with: Controlling and Dominating Behaviour

Fear of failure, and even looking like a failure, shows up in many ways. If she has people working under her, she becomes a bully. She begins to dominate others, forcing them to obey her. She will alienate her team and even friends if she does not get her way. She will raise her voice, shout at others and push them hard. If she cannot pass the pressure to others, she takes on the burden on herself, becoming a workaholic. She will forge ahead on the chosen path relentlessly, ignoring everything else, not stopping for rest or review. She will face burnout and exhaustion.

How the Veera Grows

The Veera is the most courageous among all the female archetypes. She will easily charge into battle with armour on. She will not hesitate to speak her mind. She does not care about pleasing people. She will go to great lengths to get what she wants. She is not afraid to oppose others and does not shy away from conflict. Yet, she can come across as wilful, inconsiderate and selfish in the pursuit of her own dreams.

The Veera grows by inviting compassion and softness into her life. First, she needs self-compassion. If the Veera is hard on others, she is hardest on herself. She is her own biggest critic. She needs to soften towards herself. If she is able to do this, she becomes more compassionate and considerate to the world around her. She needs to realize that life is not a battle to be won, nor is it a struggle that requires a constant churn. She can put down her weapons and allow herself some peace.

Veeras grow by listening to other voices. To do this, they need to be patient. They need to slow down and loosen their grip, knowing that things will not fall apart. I have loved reading and watching the stories of Rabindranath Tagore, both in film versions and the more recent short stories on Netflix. The story *Samapti* (Closure) is about the journey of a young, headstrong girl Mrinmayi (Meenu) to mature womanhood.

Meenu is a wilful, rebellious young Veera who steals mangoes from trees, hangs out with the boys, hates to adorn herself and refuses to toe the conventional line. She is so different from what is expected in the early twentieth-century milieu in Bengal that she is known as 'pagli' or the mad girl. Nevertheless, Apurva—a young, educated well-off man, who comes back to the village from Kolkata—is captivated by her energy and exuberance and wishes to marry her. Meenu cuts her beautiful long hair to avoid marriage, but she cannot escape fate.

'I married you because I wanted to,' says Apurva on their wedding night.

'What of my wants?' asks Meenu, the very reluctant wife and daughter-in-law.

Teen Kanya (1961), directed by Satyajit Ray, is based on *Samapti* and shows how Meenu runs away only to realize that she does care for her husband and returns. Her husband comes home after a futile search. 'How come you are here?' he asks, baffled.

'I wanted to,' admits Meenu.

'How did you come in?' he asks, since the door of the room is locked.

'By climbing a tree, but I will not do it again,' replies Meenu.

Meenu does not disown or squash her Veera nature. Instead she learns about choice, respect and concern for others. Over a period of time, Meenu learns to manage her Veera energy and grows from a petulant child to a mature woman in love.

Rumi, in the movie *Manmarziyan* (Self-Willed; 2018), is another typical Veera—feisty, impulsive, quick to anger and very focused on what she wants. In a conservative town, she sticks out like a sore thumb. Much to the dismay of her relatives, Rumi dyes her hair red and makes out brazenly with her lover, Vicky. 'Why should I ruin my life because of shame?' she asks, not really feeling shame.

There is much to admire about her courageous, devil-may-care attitude. But to grow, Rumi needs to know pain and rejection. Her long-time lover is not ready for commitment and Rumi impetuously agrees to marry whoever her family wants her to. She goes to the other extreme of marrying a total stranger, Robbie. Finally, it is Robbie's vulnerability, quiet fortitude and unquestioning acceptance that moves Rumi. She gives up Vicky, knowing that too much of the Veera energy will not help her to grow. She is ready to grow from the immature girl to a mature Veera. This involves letting go of pride, giving up anger and being considerate of others' wishes.

Veeras need to realize that embracing other energies will not diminish their fire. Their shadow powers are usually the Ma or Kanya energies which the Veera sees as a weakness or failing. It will help them channelize their own power in a better way that serves them and others well. Balancing movement with stillness, and relentlessness with rest, will lead to better health, happiness and holistic development in Veeras.

Case Studies

Nikita

Nikita is a sales manager in a financial-services firm who was referred to me for coaching. She began as a great individual performer, consistently exceeding her targets. She had built excellent relationships with clients and had initiated innovative wealth-management solutions. She was seen as a star performer and had received the fastest promotion in the firm's history.

But within six months in her new role, her boss began receiving complaints from her team members. They said she was driving them too hard, and insisted on going with them for all important sales meetings to close the deal. She had not taken the time to build any personal connect with the team members. 'She has no heart,' said one of her team members.

She began to be called 'Hitlerni' by the juniors. When her boss spoke to Nikita about this feedback, she was horrified. She thought she was only doing her job. She felt her team members did not take ownership. They did not push themselves. A couple of them were just lazy. She felt that she was carrying the entire burden of the target on her shoulders and was constantly stressed that she would fail. As a star performer, she could not afford that. As a woman leader, she could not afford to be seen as weak and feminine.

During the coaching sessons, Nikita understood that she could be effective even without being domineering. She would not lose respect or control by giving her team members more freedom and encouragement. She started appreciating their efforts more instead of only sharing her criticism. Nikita did not lose her Veera essence, but she learnt to channelize and temper her power according to her context. She realized that she could grow and achieve more only by enabling others.

Sania

I met Sania at a mentoring session I conducted for women entrepreneurs.

Sania is a typical Veera entrepreneur. She is passionate about her jewellery-design business and is keen to grow it. She has a great amount of energy, works around the clock and has little time for anything outside her work. However, despite the quality of her work and her innovative designs, she realized a while ago that her customers did not come back for further orders. She paid a digital-marketing agency to advertise on Facebook and put up posts on Instagram. She travelled to shows and put up stalls at the local Diwali Melas. She even thought of taking out advertisements in a prominent magazine. Sania had always believed that if she gave her customers great designs at excellent prices, they would come back. Despite all her efforts, her sales did not pick up as much as expected.

Nusrat, another participant in the workshop, gave her some helpful advice during the session. Nusrat was a successful home-based chef. Nusrat spent very little money on marketing but had a roaring business with repeat clients and referrals. Sania realized that she herself had little patience when it came to building long-lasting customer relationships. She was more of a hunter than a farmer, but the nature of her business required farming skills. The restless Veera in her was always looking for new things to do and chasing new ideas, plus her brusque and pushy manner had put many customers off from returning to her. In other words, she did not value or build long-term customer relationships.

After the session, Sania realized the importance of consistent calling and a high-touch approach with her clients, and was able to get more orders. Patient listening, connecting with the clients' family and understanding their needs helped her to meet her goals.

7

Rani: The Noble Queen

In an ideal world, the Rani, the noble queen, is the mistress of her domain. She reigns over her queendom with composure and conscientiousness. She is the one that family and friends go to in times of crisis. She is the efficient leader, who brings order to chaos, and stability in uncertain times. She is graceful, stately, holding herself up as a role model for others. Unlike the Veera who thrives in a battle, the Rani brings peace and prosperity in her wake.

She is the domestic goddess who runs an efficient household, knowing the exact location of every little thing. She likes making lists and plans and enjoys a sense of harmony and accomplishment by taking care of all the daily tasks in her domain. A well-made bed, a neat desk, files in their place, fresh flowers on the table and matching cups of hot tea—these give her pleasure. She feels secure and content that all is well with the world when her world is secure and stable. The Rani respects traditions and customs. She is the one who is the upholder of the rituals and rites in the family.

At work, the Rani is an efficient manager. Her files are in order, she arrives punctually for meetings and is known for her meticulous work. She uses her authority well. She has a moral responsibility for the well-being of her team. She calms irate customers and soothes ruffled feathers. She is the turnaround champion who is brought in to bring things under control. She loves her charts and organizers and timetables. She rarely misses a deadline.

As a young child, the Rani likes to play house. She is the one who sets the rules, and orders the father to go out and bring back provisions. She likes to arrange her toy furniture and is fascinated by the cooking set. She is also the one to organize the picnics and parties. The young Rani is a little bossy. She can create a fuss if the game is not played by her rules. She will sulk if she can't have her way but is not the one to get into a fight. She likes to have pleasant people about her who respect her authority. She will then take charge and ensure that everyone has a good time.

The home becomes the mature Rani's territory as well as a shelter and sanctuary for her. The Rani likes to have a Raja. She is the good companion and settles into the role of a consort very well. She sees the Raja as an ally, not her superior. Together, they rule over their kingdom, promising order and stability for all. As long as you listen to the Rani, you will be safe and protected.

The young Kanya can grow into a Rani after marriage. She lets go of her childish innocence and playfulness and takes on the role of the mistress of the household. The marriage usually makes a shift in the mental, emotional and physical states of a woman. She becomes a 'woman' from a 'girl'. Many girls make a smooth transition, even if they have not experienced the Apsara or Veera energy. This can also be the stage when the Apsara and Veera decide to settle down and move into a 'householder' role. This does not mean they give up their Veera or Apsara energy—the context for this power changes. The Apsara energy is channelled into romantic experiences with a partner or a creative pursuit. The Veera may continue to work outside the home and set challenging goals for herself, but she has another territory to manage along with the workplace. The Rani does not have to be a housewife to feel like a queen in her domain. Many Ranis find some space, a territory that is theirs, to control and rule and perform their duties per the norms of the culture and community.

Rani's Cultural Coding

The Rani as a ruler of the household has received social sanction from the Vedic ages. The housewife's ability to manage the budget, multitask between the chores, manage her husband and children's needs have all been hailed as praiseworthy. The Rani had a respected and powerful position during Vedic times. The *Atharva Veda* states, 'Hey wife! Become the queen and manager of everyone in the family of your husband' (14.1.20); and the *Yajur Veda* states, 'There are equal rights for men and women to get appointed as rulers' (20.9).

While there have been many Indian queens who have ably assisted their husbands without taking on a leadership role, history stands witness to many Ranis who have been just and able rulers in their own right. The Mughal empress Nur Jehan (1577–1645) was the power behind the throne of her husband Jahangir and issued edicts and coins in her own name. Ahilyabai Holkar, for instance, became queen of Malwa in 1767, after the death of her father-in-law, her husband and son having predeceased him. Instead of committing sati as per the prevalent practice or giving up her position, she petitioned the Peshwa to continue to rule her state from Maheshwar.

She proved to be an able queen who defended her kingdom against invaders, built several temples, forts and roads, cared for people and administered swift justice. In a time of crisis and confusion, she took charge and brought in an era of peace and prosperity. Not only was she brave, she was an astute politician and people manager. A poem written by Joanna Baillie in 1849 on Ahalyabai Holkar is testimony to how many she inspired: 'In latter days from Brahma came/To rule our land, a noble dame/Kind was her heart, and bright her fame/Ahalya was her honoured name.'

Other able queens include Razia Sultan, Chand Bibi, Rani Mangammal of Madurai (who ruled as regent until her grandson came of age) and Manikarnika of Jhansi (discussed earlier). Queens like Velu Nachiyar and Abbaka too combined the Veera and Rani energies to fight in battle and rule ably in times of peace. Most of these queens have been relegated to oblivion in our history books. They were the exception and not the rule. The rule was patriarchy eroding the Rani's authority, while leaving her responsibilities untouched.

Section XX of the 'Anusasana Parv' of the Mahabharat highlights this: Ashtavakra said, "Women can never be their own mistresses. This is the opinion of the Creator himself, viz., that a woman never deserves to be independent. There is not a single woman in the three worlds that deserves to be regarded as the mistress of her own self."[1]

Even today, millennia later, thousands of Ranis are dependents, forced to live their life in servitude. Instead of being an equal companion to the spouse, they have become servants. Since the wife is not given any position of power, she must gain protection through service to the man. The woman, especially in an unhappy marriage, is a bonded labourer who cannot break out of her shackles. In the Ramayan, when the noble queen Sita meets Anusuya (the wife of sage Atri and renowned for her chastity), they have a conversation on the role of a woman.

'Even if my husband is without fortune,' says Anusuya, 'he should be unhesitatingly obeyed by me.'

Sita agrees, 'No austerity, apart from obedience to her husband, is decreed for women,' and Anusuya blesses Sita with a garland, jewels and a body cream that never runs out, so that she can look beautiful for her husband (Ayodhya Kand, Sarga 118).

Today we see so many homes where the Rani has been reduced to a drudge. She is the bearer of the domestic load. According to the Organisation for Economic Co-operation and Development's latest statistics (*OECD.Stat*, February 2021), Indian women do nearly six hours (352 minutes) of unpaid work per day, while men do less than an hour (52 minutes). When it comes to paid work, Indian men do a little over six hours (391 minutes) daily, while women do just three hours (185 minutes) of paid work daily. India has one of the lowest rates of female workforce participation in the world. It fell from 27 per cent to 25 per cent in 2019. One of the main reasons for this is the huge amount of unpaid work that women do. The domestic load ensures that the woman is kept busy inside the four walls and finds it difficult to exert her power outside the home.

Even within the four walls, the Ranis have to jostle for power. The age-old mother-in-law vs daughter-in-law trope is well known. Two Ranis in the same territory will lead to war. Using the divide-and-rule strategy, the duo will compete for the attention and favour of the power centre—the man of the house. Typically, the older Rani, who has already established her rule, is reluctant to hand over the reins to the new queen. Sometimes, she gracefully gives in and takes a backseat, but more often it is the new Rani who finds other areas to assert her authority and yields control in the home. I know many working women who invoke their Rani energy at work and leave the running of the household to the mother-in-law. The nuclear family structure has, to some extent, resolved this issue, with separate territories for each Rani.

The Rani's power has been eroded by making her believe that she has very little power. Many women who do not work outside the home, refer to themselves as 'just a housewife'. A friend confessed that her eight-year-old daughter did not want to tell her classmates that her mother was a housewife, so she told them she was a dress designer. My friend does have a great interest in designing lovely clothes for herself and her children, and choosing the materials and accessories, but has not made a profession of it.

In the movie *English-Vinglish* (2012), the mother, Shashi (played by the late Sridevi), does not feel respected by her husband or children even though she has a thriving business making laddus from home. Her inability to speak good English is one of the reasons for their disregard. Shashi herself lacks confidence and does not own her Rani power as an equal head of the household.

Rani's Relationships

The Rani sees men as her allies. She wants a good companion who will respect her and be worthy of her. As a wife, mother and mother-in-law, her relationship with the man is important for her. Ranis who feel insecure in their position forge relationships with men seeing them as means to consolidate their power. Unlike the Apsara, the Rani will not seduce a man with her charm or sexual energy. She prefers to forge strategic alliances or use her influencing skills to get the men in power to her side.

The Rani is also more pragmatic than a Kanya or Apsara in her choice of partner. She is influenced by practical factors rather than just romantic dreams. She looks for a man who will be a good provider and a good father to their children. She will choose the responsible and respectable man over the swashbuckling Romeo. This does not mean she does not want love or romance. Her love is the pleasant calm love guided by her values rather than giddy attraction. She is quite happy to have an arranged marriage and make sure that a potential husband ticks off all the boxes. She dreams of a good life with a home, children and a good man beside her.

In Jane Austen's 1811 masterpiece, Sense and Sensibility, I see Elinor Dashwood as the Rani and not Marianne. I saw the Tamil film version, the sumptuously made *Kandukondain Kandukondain* (I have seen it, I have seen it; 2000), where Sowmya (played by Tabu) the sensible sister is willing to give up her romance to get a respectable job and do her duty. The Rani may even view love with an unsuitable man as being dangerous. She is habitually risk-averse unless she also has a strong Veera streak, in which case the Rani and Veera face-off in an internal conflict. This internal conflict leads to confusion and unhappiness which needs to be resolved soon.

Lata Mehra, the heroine of Vikram Seth's magnificent novel, *A Suitable Boy*, first falls in love with a Muslim boy, Kabir Durrani. Lata is intelligent, outspoken and shows many aspects of the Veera energy. Yet, she also has a Rani energy which favours stability and calmness over rebellious disruption.

She eventually decides to marry Haresh Khanna, the 'suitable boy' from the same caste, whom her mother approves of (Seth 1993).

Many Apsaras who have been able to experiment with relationships in their youth, or have experienced unsatisfactory love affairs often invoke their Rani energy later in life and settle down with their suitable boy. The beautiful actress Madhuri Dixit, who was at the height of her career in the eighties, gave it up and married Dr Nene, a man introduced by her brother. She left the glamour of Bollywood, for keeping home in the USA and buying groceries at the neighbourhood store. In an interview, she stated that she 'savored being a housewife' and getting up early to cook for her husband. Their relationship is based on mutual respect, give and take and a foundation of shared values. This is the Rani's ideal relationship.

Rani's Career Choices

The Rani is a valuable employee in any context. She excels at execution and brings a keen eye for detail to her role. She is good at operations and management roles. In fact, the Rani is generally good at anything she undertakes, since her sense of discipline and responsibility ensures that the job gets done. The Rani who feels called to public service makes a good administrator or project manager. Ranis are good at stable and predictable jobs and need a work environment that is structured and has clear goals. They do better in an organized, stable organization than in a start-up, but make the best employees for an entrepreneur who wishes to run the business well.

Ranis also make good lawyers. They are particular about the rule of the law and with their eye for detail, they can prepare a foolproof case. They bring a natural respect for the process and a passion for upholding social norms that serve the common good.

Ranis are usually more rational than artistic. They are not comfortable with subjects that require imagination and subjective interpretation and prefer to work with numbers and science, rather than tackling abstract concepts. Ranis can be creative and bring a keen eye and discipline to their craft. A Rani friend is excellent at copying the work of her favourite artists but not ready to experiment with her own designs. Ranis will complete that painting and finish that book without getting distracted. They need a definite start and finish to what they do. They also feel the need to be productive and useful and to see tangible results in all that they do. They make good accountants and auditors who are able to pick out errors and aberrations quickly. They have an almost intuitive sense for noticing anything that is unusual, strange or incorrect. They bring the same keen eye to running a home. Ranis who choose to be homemakers will happily take on the responsibility and keep an immaculate household humming smoothly.

Rani as a Leader

The Rani welcomes the opportunity to take on the leadership role. She likes to know her responsibilities and is particular about her territory and her people. The Rani does not need to be in the limelight as long as the work gets done.

The Rani needs an SOP—a standard operating procedure—for her operations. If there isn't any, she will create one. She is an ethical leader who plays by the rules. She is meticulous and rigorous. She is punctual and her meetings usually run on time. She does not like frivolous chit-chat or indulge in it, is correct in her dealings, and has a strong task-focus. The Rani is respected by her team members who are awed by her razor-sharp eye for error and detail. The Rani can be a good teacher and will happily take team members under her wing and train them to be like her. The Rani can happily rule for a long time and as long there is no major upheaval, she will bring in profits and plaudits for the organization.

The Rani is a good strategist and planner. Planning, forecasting and envisaging scenarios are her strengths. If she is in politics, the Rani will know how to play the game, how to forge alliances and manage a campaign. A leader with an over-abundant Rani energy can become an overbearing perfectionist. Her team members may feel stifled and stressed because she demands high quality and seems to have unreasonable standards. A Rani leader who is able to tap into her innate strengths and balance her dominant Rani energy with the energies of the other archetypes will be extremely successful.

INDRA NOOYI: THE RANI WHO RULED PEPSICO

Indra Nooyi, former chairman of PepsiCo, is one of the most powerful women in the world. Her core energy is that of the Rani, though she has invoked the Veera energy as per her need. Indra Nooyi's presence is that of a smart, down-to-earth, no-nonsense woman. She held many offices during the course of her long career at PepsiCo, including as president and chief financial officer (CFO), before going on to become chairman and CEO, and eventually rising to become chairman. She had also earlier worked with the Boston Consulting Group (BCG) as an international corporate strategist.

In an interview at the Forbes Women Summit, Nooyi admitted that her strategy to succeed as a brown immigrant woman in America was to be better than anybody else at anything she did.

She has been quoted as saying, 'Whatever you do, throw yourself into it. Throw your head, heart and hand to it.' She was known for her flawless execution and has been described as a perfectionist. A profile of Indra Nooyi in *Fortune* magazine describes a market visit she made to a store in Chicago. Nooyi noticed every little detail—even the fact that the two halves of the Pepsi logo did not align and one can of Pepsi was missing from a shelf. She has said, 'I pick up the details that make an organization insane. But sweating the details is more important that anything else.' Before taking any decision, she does her homework thoroughly. Whether it was the divestment of the restaurant business or the acquisition of Quaker Oats, Nooyi needed to completely prepared before committing to the decision. She spent the weekend reading ten books and speaking to professors to understand the IT system completely before taking the decision to change it.

During her stint in BCG, Indra Nooyi learnt to create frameworks that served the client and was passionate about being a lifelong student, learning and absorbing everything.

Nooyi is known to be a great strategist. She has great foresight and plans accordingly. While at PepsiCo she coined the slogan 'Performance with Purpose' and devised a strategy that marked a significant shift from the kind of products that PepsiCo produced. She was concerned about PepsiCo's contribution to health issues and water usage. Under her leadership, PepsiCo shifted its focus from sugary colas and fried snacks to healthier products like Quaker Oats. Her foresight and ability to solve problems from a long-term perspective made her one of the most successful CEOs at PepsiCo.

Indra Nooyi spent twenty-four years at PepsiCo, twelve of these as its chairman and CEO. She is one of most respected leaders in the world. She has been able to leverage her Rani power without falling into its traps and also be guided by her values of commitment, contribution and connection.

Rani's Power Source: The Drive for Perfection

The Rani derives her power from her desire for excellence and perfection, and from being disciplined and orderly. The Rani sees perfection both as an end in itself and a means of bringing stability and prosperity to the world. The world does not thrive in chaos. The universe has to function according to its laws. She can bring order out of chaos by doing her job really well.

The Rani's core strengths stem from her clear-eyed view of the world, her discernment, meticulousness and stable presence. She stands firm when all about her are scared and disturbed. She brings her calm presence and restores order and sanity in an uncertain world.

Rani's Core Needs: Order and Stability

The Rani needs to know that everything is alright. All her efforts go to establish the correct order in the world, that is, whatever she considers her domain. It could be the house, her work or her children. Whatever is in her charge has to be absolutely perfect. She may not be worried about what she considers outside her circle of concern, though ideally she would like to control everything. But the pragmatic Rani knows that many things in the world are unpredictable and uncertain, therefore it is even more important to bring what she can under her power.

The Rani upholds traditions because they bring a sense of order and continuity in her world. She does not like to go against the norm unless there are very good reasons. She is the custodian of the conduct of the community. Anusuya, the respected wife of sage Atri, was the guardian of the social norms of her time. This is why Sita had approached her for guidance. Anusuya's power was derived from her pious observances. Many Rani women are religious and particular about following a system of practices as a way of perpetuating long-standing customs.

Rani's Power Blocks

The Rani is unable to realize her full power if she allows her needs to overwhelm her. An excess of Rani energy and the inability to involve other energies create blocks for the Rani.

The Rani who feels insecure and frustrated and becomes overbearing shows the dark side of the Rani power.

Emotionally Drained by: Anxiety

Ranis tend to be worrywarts and live in a perpetual state of anxiety. Ranis who are not able to balance and overcome this feeling of nervousness and worry can have panic attacks and health issues. They imagine the worst-case scenario and expect it to happen. Many Ranis live with a sense of unease, always believing that if anything can go wrong, it will. They prepare contingency plans, but never feel completely reassured.

Many Ranis find that they are unable to enjoy the simple pleasures of life because of this tendency to worry. While this makes them great planners, it also makes them killjoys. They always expect rain to spoil their picnic and spend their time looking for that dark cloud instead of enjoying the day. This anxiety makes them poor companions on a holiday. Their tendency to be overcautious can be irritating for those who have a higher risk-threshold.

Fears: Loss of Control

The Rani fears chaos more than anything else. Many Ranis cannot handle sudden change. A chaotic situation is unpredictable and she will have no control in such a situation. She fears losing control of her emotions. She needs to relax her grip on her life and emotions, to loosen up and meet life head-on. Sometimes, the Rani gets a companion who helps her to do this. It could be a spouse, a friend or even her own children.

Responds with: Judging, Controlling or Withdrawing

The Rani masks her anxieties and insecurities by a tendency to be judgemental. Her strong preconceived notions help her to make decisions and navigate the uncertain world. But these judgements keep her from new connections and new possibilities. Ranis always see the world in black and white and tend to ignore the many shades and complexities in between.

A high-stress situation can bring out the best in a Rani, and the worst. The fear makes her more cautious, fearful, risk-averse and controlling. The Rani who cannot manage her fears and use her powers will become fretful, volatile and a terror to be around. She will try to control everyone around her. The more tightly she tries to hold herself and the reins, the more stressed she feels. Other Ranis may just shut-down and become completely passive. They will be frozen like deer caught in the headlights, unable to take the steps that will get them to safety.

How the Rani Grows

The Rani grows by actively welcoming change and letting go of her need to control everything. She needs to step out of her routine, experiment with new things, take risks and put herself out there.

In the move *Qarib Qarib Single* (2017), the heroine Jaya (played by Malayalam actress Parvathy) is a quiet Rani whose life is clean, well-ordered and predictable. Since the death of her husband, Jaya has become a workaholic, ruling her workplace firmly and kindly like a true queen. She is unwilling to take any risk in her personal life and seems quite content with a sedate routine. Yet she feels the need for a companion and enrols in a dating website. After a slew of unsuitable characters, Jaya meets Yogi, endearingly played by Irfan Khan. Yogi is everything that Jaya is not—spontaneous, sloppy, colorful and annoying. She embarks on an adventure with him, ostensibly to meet his ex-girlfriends. This is completely unlike her character and she is filled with trepidation and excitement.

It is this strange and unpredictable journey that helps Jaya to grow and become open to new experiences. Jaya—who always planned her day, refused to share her water, wore only pastels and never did anything crazy—now discovers a new side to her own personality. She does not give up her Rani energy, but learns to embrace her Apsara and Veera energies too which are usually her shadow powers. She also discovers the light-hearted playfulness of the Kanya and in the end becomes a more confident and interesting person.

The Rani similarly needs to step out of her comfort zone and break her routine. The Rani is great at managing chaos outside. She will give sage advice on handling messy affairs and messy rooms, and is the go-to person to manage your crises, but she does not open herself up to others easily. She needs to get past her judgement of others and embrace those who are different and unlike herself, without trying to order their lives. This is her challenge and her area of growth. If she can treat disruptions as learning experiences and take measured risks with preparation, she can grow into her full power.

Case Studies

Mamta

Mamta, a participant in a leadership workshop, narrated this story during a session on Comfort Zone. Mamta was a quality-assurance manager in a company that manufactured automobile parts. She was one of the few women in senior management. Mamta had been in this role for eight years, growing the function from a one-woman division to a five-member team. The senior managers respected her expertise and ability to spot defects as well as potential problems. Mamta's team looked up to her and followed her directions unquestioningly. They knew that she would never steer them in the wrong direction. The two women in her team wanted to be just like her—always calm, composed and who knew the answer to everything. Her team members didn't really know Mamta personally, since she drew a clear line between professional and personal space. I could sense that Mamta was a Rani.

After the retirement of the current operations director, the position had become open. Mamta and her colleague Ashraf, the operations manager, were in the running. One part of Mamta wanted the promotion, along with increased status and pay. Yet another part of her did not. She was known as the 'queen of quality' in the company, a position that she had earned through hard work and determination. She did not think anyone in her team was ready to take on her role. The role of the operations director involved dealing with the union at the factory, managing the workforce, handling all kinds of emergencies, like the time when they had to stop production due to a fire. She was not sure that she wanted to take on all that responsibility. What if she could not cope? What if the workers went on strike?

Finally Mamta decided to let someone else handle all the hassle that came with the senior role. She preferred to focus on her current role where she had a great reputation and an excellent track record. She also felt there was so much she could still do in the field of quality. When the CEO asked her, Mamta did not express interest.

Mamta, like many Ranis, was apprehensive about change and ambiguity. She did not want to lose her territory and her fear of the unknown led her to stay in her safe and orderly comfort zone.

Mamta continued as quality-assurance manager for the next year. Ashraf became her boss and after a while it became difficult for her to report to him. She felt she was much more qualified for the role in terms of knowledge and competence. The operations continued smoothly. There were no strikes. Ashraf had learnt quickly, building a good relationship with the head of the union. Why hadn't she said yes to the position!

Mamta would regret that decision for the rest of her career. Her need for stability had been her strength, but it also came in the way of her growth. She realized the impact of the missed opportunity. A year later, she did step out of her comfort zone and signed up for an Executive MBA programme. She was initially very apprehensive about this step, but the experience of managing her work, home and the programme gave her the confidence to take more risks. She leveraged her Rani power to structure her life and manage her schedule, and benefited personally and professionally from the management programme.

Two years after she secured her MBA degree, Mamta received an offer from another company as operations head. Though the company was smaller than her current employer, Mamta took up the opportunity. She excelled in her new role. The smaller size of the organization gave her more opportunity to try new things. Mamta also began mentoring younger women in the new company. 'You should put up your hand for bigger roles and challenging projects. Step out of your comfort zone,' she would tell them.

Andrea

Andrea shared this story during a virtual open workshop for women. Andrea was a wonderful homemaker with two teenage daughters and a caring husband. She and her husband had first met as hotel management students. Her husband became a chef at a prominent restaurant in Mumbai. After marriage and two children, Andrea quit her demanding career in the hospitality industry. She channelized her passion into her household. Everything in her home worked well—there were always fresh flowers on the table, the pantry was well stocked, the marble floors gleamed and everything was spotlessly clean. She had a daily routine that ran like clockwork and she was the one who planned the family holidays. She would research the best fares and go through all the Tripadvisor reviews before choosing a place that met the entire family's requirements.

Then, in March 2020, her life was completely thrown off-track, thanks to the coronavirus outbreak. Suddenly, her children were home since schools were closed. Restaurants shut down and her husband had no job. The pandemic left Andrea even more anxious than usual. She refused to let her daughters step out of their apartment and go down to the park. The prospect of infection filled her with dread. She could not sleep at night. She would get up and start cleaning some part of the house. She started cleaning everything that came into their house with antibacterial wipes.

She snapped at her family members when they questioned her actions, and felt that they were taking the pandemic too lightly. She felt exhausted and within two weeks of the lockdown, her nerves were frayed and her blood pressure had spiked. She worried about the future and about her husband's job prospects. She wanted him to go out of the house and look for another job, but she was also scared of the infection he might bring back with him. Andrea needed to take anti-anxiety medication to get some respite. She was unable to articulate her fears and felt helpless at the uncertainty of the future.

Then her mother was diagnosed with breast cancer, and Andrea felt that her world had collapsed around her. She decided to leave for Goa with her daughters to care for her mother. The initial days were a struggle but the sense of responsibility she felt for her family brought out the best of Andrea. She also connected to her Ma energy and became the primary caregiver for her parents and daughters. She structured everyone's schedules, organized the hospital visits and maintained a strict safety regime at home. The sense of being needed by others helped her to overcome her anxiety and pull herself together.

8

Ma: The Nurturing Caregiver

'The ideal of womanhood in India is motherhood—that marvellous, unselfish, all-suffering, ever forgiving mother,' said Swami Vivekananda at a lecture he gave in Pasadena, USA (Vivekananda, 1900).

The *Ma* is one of the most common and revered female archetypes across the world. It is present within both genders as the creative, regenerative force that gives birth to new thoughts, new ideas, new projects that nurtures them to fruition. But the *Ma* archetype lives in its full power in women.

Greek goddesses Gaia and Demeter, the Asian goddess of compassion and mercy Kwan Yin, and the mother goddess worshipped in many ancient cultures, all symbolize the power of the Great Mother. In fact, Carl Jung stated that the mother archetype is a part of our collective subconscious. She symbolizes fertility, creation, rebirth, the bountiful harvest as well as the destruction of evil. She is the earth that holds the seeds of life in her womb, she is the earth who bestows a bountiful harvest on her children, she is also the earth who can swallow a city whole.

During her childhood, the Ma likes to play house, likes to cook with her little pots and pans and feed her siblings small makeshift meals of leaves and pebbles. She slips with ease into the role of the mother who stays at home while the father goes to work. Young girls in India are thrust into the Ma role at an early age, as they end up caring for their younger siblings when the mother goes out to work. The young Ma does not mind this. She is usually the elder daughter who becomes a surrogate mother at home, enjoying not only the responsibility but also the joy of bossing over her younger siblings. She also fetches and carries for her mother and is quite adept at household chores.

As a grown woman, the Ma retains her innate desire to provide sustenance and succour to others. She does this even if she is not the biological mother. The Ma is the woman who loves to cook and feed people, whose home is always fragrant with the smell of food and fresh flowers. There is something generous and welcoming about her smile. You want to tell her your troubles knowing that she will soothe you with a warm drink and warm hug. She is abundant. She is selfless. She will sacrifice everything for the sake of those she loves. At her best, she is a loving, caring woman who wants nothing more than to be with her loved ones and take care of them.

Ma's Cultural Coding

Remember Indian movies from a few decades ago? The ideal mother was often a widowed lady whose only aim in life was to bring up her children well. She took on the role of the dead father, she forswore any sexual intimacy and focused all her energies on her role as provider and caregiver.

The late actress Nargis in the film (and as) *Mother India* (1957) was a metonymic representation of the Indian woman who was moral, selfless and sacrificing. She was the last one to eat in her family, she dressed in a ragged sari so that her children would have new clothes, she took on any menial task or hard labour to make ends meet. She was the North Star, the moral compass of the family and entire village. The filmi Ma was usually the epitome of endurance and suffering, unless her children were threatened. Then she would become Kali Ma and reduce her enemies to ashes.

Our culture celebrates, venerates and glorifies the ideal Ma. This notion of Ma is closely linked to a woman's identity as a biological mother. This mother is defined by her children, just as children are created by the mother. This notion of the ideal mother is so strong and so firmly entrenched that many women feel compelled to live up to this image even if the Ma energy is not alive in them.

Mothers who follow the mother code are worshipped, venerated and elevated on a pedestal. They become the Mother Goddess. The *Manusmriti* states, 'From the point of view of reverence due/a teacher is tenfold superior to a mere lecturer/a father is a hundredfold superior to a teacher/and a mother is a thousandfold superior to a father.'

Mothers who don't follow the mother code are vilified, killed, ostracized and written out of history. The sage Jamadagni ordered his sons to kill their mother Renuka. Her fault? She gazed a little too long at a handsome prince sporting in the river, and didn't come back on time with her pot of water! Another case is that of the impatient mother-to-be Gandhari, wife of the blind King Dhritarashtra, who smote her pregnant stomach with angry fists. Instead of children, she delivered a lump of flesh. Thanks to the boon of a sage, the lump, cut into a hundred pieces and incubated in pots of clarified butter, became the hundred Kauravas. The hundred Kaurava brothers are the villains of the great epic, the Mahabharat, and were defeated by their five cousins, the Pandavas.

The Ma's primary relationship is with the child. In the Indian context, the most important relationship is that of the mother with the son. All our epics and myths glorify the woman who has a son. Her power and status derive from her ability to birth boys. Kaushalya is venerated as the mother of Rama, Kunti is known as the mother of the five Pandavas, and Yashoda is lovingly remembered as the mother of naughty little baby Krishna. The relationship between mothers and daughters is absent in all these stories.

In some versions of the story of Rama, we learn that Kaushalya had a daughter called Shanta before the birth of Rama (and the other three brothers from other queens). Shanta was given away in adoption and later married to Rishi Rishyasringa, so that he would perform a yagna to bring forth sons for Dashrath. The Pandavas' mother, Kunti, was born to King Shurasen but was given in adoption to her uncle, King Kuntibhoj. We do not know what the mothers felt about being parted from their daughters. Their value, however, lay in their ability to birth sons.

The Ma has a symbiotic relationship with her son. He needs her first as a young child and then she needs him in her old age. The Ma loves her son but she also sees him as the golden ticket. The mother nourishes and provides for her son. In return, he worships her and takes care of her.

The mother and daughter have a primal relationship. Each is a part of the other. The mother lives through her sons but lives on in her daughters. The mother loves her daughters but her main concern is to preserve and protect them. The daughter is always seen as 'paraya dhan' (borrowed wealth) that one day will be handed over to the rightful owner (the husband). The mother is too afraid to invest her emotions fully in her daughter.

My parents had only two daughters. I never felt discriminated or unloved because of my gender. My mother, who is a staunch feminist and also a traditional mother, brought me and my sister up carefully, with injunctions for our physical safety but also gave us the freedom to follow our own path. I have one child. My daughter is more than enough for me. I have no regrets about not having a son.

However, the practice of discriminating against daughters is prevalent even today. One of my house-helps used to save money to buy eggs for her son but her two daughters would not be allowed this luxury. Simi, one of the ladies I coached, related a story when her mother would allow her younger brother to stay out later in the evening to play but she would be summoned home by 5 p.m. Her brother would get new clothes more often than she did. Simi would be given his half-used pencils, while he would get new ones. Ironically, the brother moved to the USA and Simi moved to the same building as her parents and took care of them even after her marriage. The brother visited once a year, but the mother still had a soft spot for him.

In a patriarchal culture, the Ma derives her power from the male she cares for. She sees this tilt towards the male offspring as necessary for her own survival.

Ma's Relationships

The Ma seeks a relationship with a partner who needs her, who she can pamper. She is the one who will go out of her way in the relationship. As a girlfriend, she is the one who will cook his favourite foods, buy him a shirt in his favourite colour and remember his dentist appointment. She will call her partner 'baby'; it's not just as a term of endearment. To her he feels like a baby to be loved and taken care of.

Acts of service make up her language of love. She is the wife who will admit to her girlfriends, 'Uff, he can't do anything by himself. I have to pack his suitcase/give him his pills/wash his shirts.' She says this with an indulgent smile, relishing the little things she can do for her partner. She does this naturally and effortlessly. She does not expect anything in return, except to be cherished and needed. 'You do so much for me. How will I manage without you?' is music to her ears.

The Ma as a friend is devoted and loyal. She is the girl in your hostel who always has some food in her room for others to share. She will stay back and take care of a sick roommate, she will bring back thoughtful little gifts for others after her holidays and is always there as a shoulder to cry on.

Sometimes, the Ma feels that she is being taken for granted. Sometimes, she gets tired of just giving and giving. She may be too used up and exhausted. 'You rest,' her husband will tell her, maybe on Mother's Day. 'We will cook and clean and take you out and pamper you.' The Ma enjoys this for a day. She cannot take too much pampering. She needs to get back to her role of primary caregiver.

Ma's Career Choices

The woman with a strong Ma energy excels in careers where she can work in a small group with deep connections. She works well in not-for-profit organizations, where she has a chance to contribute and feel valued. She makes for a caring doctor or nurse. She is the home-based chef who wants everyone to love her food and will have that personal touch when dealing with her customers. She will make a good counsellor or a patient teacher, who genuinely cares for her students. She will remember their names and will be interested in their lives.

The Ma does not like a high-pressure, very task-focused, impersonal work environment. She needs to feel that she makes a difference and that she is a valued member of the team. Monetary rewards alone don't motivate her. The way to retain her is through loyalty and inclusion. The Ma works best in a high-touch environment where she is seen and connected to others. She does not want to be left alone to do her work. Her work is through other people and with other people.

Ma as a Leader

The Ma may not be a born leader but she does not shy away from a leadership role. She will gladly take on the mantle of the leader to serve her followers. She will sacrifice her own happiness for the sake of her 'children' and her identity is defined by those under her care. She is loving, generous and usually says 'my guys', 'my family', or 'my kids' when referring to her team. She will stand by them, no matter what. If she feels that her team is immature or not yet capable, she will take the burden of responsibility on her shoulders. She brings goodies for her team after travel and often invites them for a home-cooked meal. Team development and growth is important for her and she can be a great coach and mentor. As a leader, she believes she knows what is best for the organization.

The Ma as a leader will be surprised and hurt if a team member raises his voice against her. After all, she is doing everything for their benefit! She will fiercely protect her people against others and expects loyalty and devotion. She will go to war to save those she thinks of as her own and may even alienate the higher authorities for their sake. Sometimes, the Ma's relationship focus can come in the way of her task orientation. She will hesitate to tick off non-performers and take tough decisions that go against her people.

J. JAYALALITHAA: GLAMOUR GIRL TO MOTHER GODDESS

My first glimpse of the late Jayalalithaa was in a black-and-white movie on television. She was a beautiful buxom woman with a bouffant hairdo, shimmying away in a tight dress, making eyes at the hero, coy one minute and seductive the next. It was difficult to imagine that this young woman, described as 'kavarchi kanni' (glamour girl), would become a political leader.

Jayalalithaa swiftly rose to power as the protégé and trusted confidante of M.G. Ramachandran (better known as MGR), her one-time leading man and later chief minister of Tamil Nadu. She became the propaganda secretary of the All India Anna Dravida Munnetra Kazhagam (AIADMK) party, and much to the dismay of male career politicians, showed no signs of quitting politics.

Jayalalithaa was not a born Ma. She described herself as a naïve, shy, innocent Kanya who was thrust into the limelight through films and then politics. In an interview with Simi Garewal on the latter's talk show, I heard Jayalalithaa say that she wanted to become a lawyer or an academician. It was the Kanya's need for acceptance and desire to earn the love of her mother that propelled her to a successful career in films. It was her desire to please her mentor and guide MGR that led her to politics. She could not say no to either of them.

The death of her mentor, MGR, proved to be a significant milestone in Jayalalithaa's life. Party workers prevailed upon her to accept a leadership position in the AIADMK, which was orphaned after the death of its charismatic leader. Despite misgivings, Jayalalithaa agreed. She survived a brutal struggle for power and emerged as the leader of the AIADMK, besting MGR's wife, Janaki. A shocking incident in 1989—where she was assaulted, beaten and jailed—saw her transformation from Kanya to Ma.

As a leader in a patriarchal, chauvinistic culture, she could no longer be the Kanya. She was neither the daughter nor the wife or widow of a leader. She could not be seen as the Apsara, a single beautiful woman. She had already been vilified for being hot-headed and arrogant and called 'puratchi thalaivi' (rebel leader). To emerge successful in the political climate of Tamil Nadu, Jayalalithaa had to become the Ma of all—Amma.

It was a transformed Jayalalithaa who took the oath as chief minister in 1991, just two years after the attack on her. Gone was the naïve young girl. She had put on weight and now appeared almost matronly. She now always appeared in public with a large cape draped over her sari, hiding any signs of vulnerability and femininity. She was a literally and figuratively a larger-than-life figure. This was the Ma energy that she tapped into consciously and subconsciously for the rest of her career.

Jayalalithaa became a champion for women as she started a Cradle Baby scheme to root out female foeticide and infanticide. Unwanted girl babies could be placed in a cradle kept at government hospitals, at primary health centres (PHCs) and outside orphanages, and the state would arrange for legal adoptions. She launched a slew of populist schemes aimed at alleviating the suffering of the poor and underprivileged. She fed them through the 'Amma Canteens' that served a nourishing meal for just a few rupees and quenched their thirst with the 'Amma Drinking Water' schemes that provided affordable water for the poor.

As the caring benign Ma who always thought of the welfare of her children, she soon became not just any mother, but Amma, the powerful mother goddess who was worshipped by her children, the people of Tamil Nadu. She could now be high-handed and whimsical, punishing those who opposed her, while blessing loyal devotees who prostrated themselves on the ground in front of her and sought her favour.

Jayalalithaa died in 2016 after a serious illness. The party was lost without her at the helm. She had not created any successor. Nobody could fill her slippers. Ten days after her death, a party worker started building a temple in her name, in Thanjavur in Tamil Nadu. The temple has framed photographs and a bronze bust of Amma. In 2019, a shrine honouring her was built inside another temple in Coimbatore.

Dayal Kumar, an AIADMK worker in Coimbatore says, 'We have built a temple for her in honour of her service to the people in this area. She sacrificed her lifetime for us and she is considered a God who can be seen' (*The News Minute*, 2019).

The mother goddess lives on.

Ma's Power Sources: Fostering Connections and Sustaining Relationships

The *Atharva Veda* states, 'We want tremendous power. Hence we please the motherly pure woman with our noble words and actions. She is as patient as the wide sky. She shall remove our miseries and provide us shelter in all situations' (7.6.4).

This powerful Ma who makes the impossible happen through her love and faith is a common leitmotif in our culture. The magic of the Ma is even more powerful than that of the chaste woman. The Mother's word is law. Her wishes are paramount.

Remember that scene in the famous movie *Deewar* (Wall; 1975) when two brothers find themselves on either sides of the law. Vijay is a criminal who has accumulated property, cars and a hefty bank balance. He taunts his police-officer brother Ravi, asking him what he has except his rented quarters and two sets of uniforms. 'I have Ma,' replies Ravi, quashing any further response.

Of course the virtuous brother, blessed by the Ma for being upright and good, wins over the 'bad' brother. The Ma here is not just a caregiver, but also in many ways the guardian of social mores and righteous values. She is seen as the upholder of the culture and traditions. Her faith and belief in her sons, can even ensure that they reincarnate after an untimely death to avenge her—as seen in the Hindi film *Karan Arjun* (1995). Two boys, born in different parts of the country, are brought together by fate to fight the evil villains who have imprisoned the noble mother. No Bollywood fan can forget the actress Rakhee (who played the mother) saying 'Mere Karan Arjun aayenge' (My Karan Arjun will come). The two strapping lads descend on the villains, wreck havoc and after some good-old 'dishum dishum', they free their mother-from-a-past-life.

The blessings of the Ma, even her mere presence, can bestow power upon those near her. The Ma has an enormous impact on the child she births and brings up. A research study led by Dr Joan Luby, a professor of child psychiatry at Washington University School of Medicine, revealed that a nurturing mother causes an increase in the size of the hippocampus, that part of the brain which is 'important for learning memory and stress responses'. Dr Luby says, 'It's now clear that a caregiver's nurturing is not only good for the development of the child, but it actually physically changes the brain' (Castro, 2012).

In his book *The Great Mother*, Eric Neumann, the Jungian analyst, explains that the Great Mother has two positive aspects. The first aspect of her power is her ability to nourish and protect, to give care, warmth and love. The other transformative characteristic is the urge towards change, growth and creativity (Neumann 1991).

The Ma can have a great positive influence on her 'children', all those she takes under her wing. A powerful Ma, who is secure in her position and feels a strong sense of connection to her group, will go out of her way to grow and support them. Her ability to foster deep connections and sustain long-term relationships is her core strength. A Ma with the creative urge is excellent at initiating change in organizations. If she can combine her strong nurturing skills with the creative drive, she can become a force to reckon with.

Ma's Core Need: Belonging

The Ma, like all of us, wants belonging and connection. She gets this by being needed, by serving and helping others so that they will continue to need her. Sometimes, this deep desire to be needed becomes the overarching purpose of her life and she is willing to suspend her own needs in the service of others. The sweetest moment in a mother's life is just after the birth of her child. She loves her small helpless baby with a fierce intensity. This baby needs her like no one else ever will. The hungry pull of the infant at her breast fills her with great joy. This is what the Ma believes she was made for—to give her body and soul in the service of life. The Ma continues to work hard and makes herself indispensable.

The Ma as a friend or partner is the giver in the relationship. She will be the one to reach out and call. She is happy when people reach out to her for help. She will apologize and make up in case of a conflict. She does not want to lose the connection. She will sacrifice her time and her needs so that she can bask in the glory of her goodness and generosity. She does this subconsciously, without an overt desire to secure her relationship. She is only meeting her own needs.

Ma's Power Blocks

Jungian analyst Marion Woodman calls the most negative aspect of the Mother archetype the Death Mother. The Death Mother complex reflects the devaluing of the transformative aspects of the feminine, which includes our ability to sustain relationships. The Death Mother is devastating because she damages successive generations of her children. The Ma's positive image and influence is vitally important to us. If this Ma is neglectful, cruel, judging, abusive and full of negativity, she leaves wounds that never heal.

A neglectful caregiver who does not perform his/her role is not just harmful for the children but for the entire community. Since this role is understood to be the sole responsibility of a woman in most societies, the term 'working mother' is fraught with tension. Without this critical role, the entire society is doomed to chaos and anarchy. Mothers who work outside the home are often torn apart by seemingly conflicting loyalties—to the children at home who she leaves behind and those at work who also need her.

Emotionally Drained by: Guilt

I do feel guilty if I sneak a chocolate when I am supposed to be in my 'mindful eating' phase. I feel guilty after a bout of 'unnecessary' shopping. Most women do feel guilty about something or the other. The Ma measures her worth through the value she brings to her relationships. This value usually involves doing various things that make her feel needed and ensure her indispensability. But the Ma is forever toggling between feeling guilty and feeling momentarily reassured.

During a workshop to prepare mothers to re-enter the workplace, I heard many stories relating to this dilemma.

- 'I sent my eight-month-old baby to day-care and went back to work,' confessed a young mother. Her eyes became moist and she flinched as though she expected the other women to pelt her with stones, each heavy with the words 'Bad Mother'. 'I can't do it again for the second one.'
- 'Why don't fathers feel any guilt leaving their children and going for work?', pondered another mother, who had quit her job to take care of the children. She seethed with suppressed rage and resentment.
- 'I feel so bad and keep worrying every time I travel away from home on work. If anything goes wrong with the children, they will blame the mother only, na?'

Guilt by itself is not a bad emotion. It is a sign that we have a conscience, that we feel responsibility towards another and is an indication that we still belong to the human race. A healthy dose of guilt makes us stick to that diet, prevents us from splurging on that horrendously expensive designer outfit that we don't need, and nudges us to relook at our moral compass.

All mothers experience some form of guilt—'my baby does not sleep at night, I must have eaten the wrong kind of food during pregnancy'; 'my child does not get a gold star, I should have watched those Baby Einstein videos instead of taking afternoon naps.' It is normal to indulge in a bout of self-flagellation. All mothers go on guilt trips. A mother's excessive guilt can become a nasty mutant that gnaws away at our vitals, diminishes our self-worth, distances us from our closest connections and often renders us incapable of coherent thought or action.

The Ma's way of coping with guilt is to over-compensate. She becomes either abjectly apologetic and panders to everyone's needs, or becomes overbearing in an attempt to take over and do everything. 'Leave it, I will do it,' says the Ma. This is not because she wants to do the task but because she will feel bad if she doesn't do it. Somehow, inaction will diminish her. She will then work herself to the point of exhaustion, her energy and vitality draining away from her. Then, she will wonder why she is not appreciated by others. After all, she is doing everything for them.

Fears: Loneliness

The Ma's biggest fear is that of loneliness and disconnection. One of the reasons she continues to sacrifice despite feeling resentful is the deep fear that she may lose the people she needs. Just as a baby fears abandonment by the mother, the Ma grows up fearing abandonment by those she loves.

The Ma who strives to become indispensable realizes that she is also dependent on the validation and presence of others. She works hard to be needed, to provide care and warmth. If the Ma does this out of pure love instead of fear, she may not feel resentful and may also be able to deal with loss of connection.

Responds with: Resentment and Smothering

The Ma is often caught up in a vicious cycle of guilt and resentment. She will sacrifice for her loved ones and tribe, out of a curious mixture of love and guilt. A Ma is expected to sacrifice, to put her needs below that of the others. She will for a while feel noble and virtuous in her sacrifice and revel in being the martyr. At a point of time, her sacrifice will lead to resentment—'I am always the one who...'; 'they don't see me or care for me...'— and she begins to feel used, taken for granted, but is too caught up in the downward spiral to get out of it.

In the Hindi movie *Helicopter Eela* (2018), the overprotective single mother of a teenage boy joins his college to keep an eye on him. 'You won't leave me and go, will you?' is the question she has repeatedly asked him since he was a small child. This fear of losing her son leads to a suffocating relationship leaving the son torn between love for his mother and his longing for freedom and self-determination. Eela, the mother, thinks she is cool but does not realize that her love is smothering her son and preventing him from living his life. The mother has become the smotherer.

The fear of loneliness often results in the Devouring Mother—one of the dark sides of the Ma archetype. The mother is so scared of losing her 'children' that she 'devours' them. She keeps them small, stunted and protected so that they cannot function without her. 'The Devouring Mother consumes her children psychologically and emotionally and often instils in them feelings of guilt at leaving her or becoming independent,' says Caroline Myss, a Jungian psychologist (Myss, *myss.com*).

This Ma is adept at emotional blackmail and manipulation. Several years ago, I watched a Tamil film called *Enga Chinna Raasa* (Our Little King; 1987). Even though I did not enjoy the movie, I was struck by the character of the mother. It was the first time that I had seen a mother who was cruel, mean and very different from the typical noble self-sacrificing woman one is used to seeing on screen. Later, this movie was remade as *Beta* (Son; 1992) in Hindi and went on to become a massive hit. Of course, this being an Indian movie, the wicked mother had to be the wicked stepmother. No biological mother could ever be shown to be the devouring mother.

The wicked stepmother kept the stepson illiterate and ignorant so that he would not 'grow' up and become independent. She portrayed the image of a sweet, virtuous mother while secretly trying to cheat him of his fortune. She kept him from getting married so that he would effectively remain attached to her and her alone. Now, imagine this were not a stepmother but a very normal woman who still wanted to control her children, usually the dearly beloved son.

The Devouring Mother as a team leader does not let her team members grow. She will forestall any attempt to give them new assignments. She will not delegate any important tasks to them, for fear that they will overshadow her and leave her behind. She will seem to be protecting her people, even as she prevents them from making that important presentation to the senior leaders. The Devouring Mother is so caught up in her fear that she will fail to see that she is causing resentment and dependency among those she claims to care about.

Ultimately, the Devouring Mother ensures that the very thing that she fears comes to pass. She is left behind, she is left alone.

Ajay's Story

Ajay, a young manager I met at one of my workshops, revealed that he and his wife were going through a tough time because of his domineering mother. As the only son of a typical Indian family, the pressure to 'look after' his parents was high. His father had retired early and was considered by his mother as 'useless'. The mother had taken a dislike to her daughter-in-law and would constantly taunt her and insult her parents. She would not allow her daughter-in-law to make anything for Ajay, especially Ajay's favourite dishes.

Ajay could not leave his parents since his mother 'was not keeping good health'. He was unhappy, torn between his wife and mother. During the session, he realized that every time he broached the topic of moving away with his wife, the mother would fall sick with mysterious ailments. He would immediately feel guilty about leaving her. His mother's medical tests were fine but she seemed unwell all the time. It was difficult for Ajay to realize that he was the victim of manipulation.

How the Ma Grows

The Ma grows by letting go of her need for others. This is extremely difficult for her. She cannot bear to be parted from her loved ones. Yet, if she can learn to do this with grace, she can truly live her full potential. Her worst nightmare is to be let go.

Many women do this when grown children have left the home. Women who do not embody a dominant Ma energy are able to do this easily, even with a sense of relief. But in many Indian homes, the mother continues to exert a strong influence on her children even after their marriage—especially if the son continues to live at home with the wife. The Ma is unable to relinquish her role, since it has been not just her power, but the core of her entire being.

Kaushalya, the mother of Rama, was devastated when she received the news that he had been exiled to live in the forest. According to Valmiki's Ramayan, she falls to the ground like a Saul tree felled by a woodcutter and then utters a long lament, which ends with, 'What is the use of life? Oh, Rama! With your brilliant face shining like moon! My life is useless without you. I shall accompany you to the forest like a weak cow going behind its calf' (Ayodhya Kand, Sarga 20).

How would he manage in the forest? How could a prince who had been used to the best of food and comfort manage on roots and raw meat in a hut? She would take care of him there in a way that Sita never could. Kaushalya could not bear to be parted from her son, though he was a grown man with a wife.

Rama had to remind his mother of her role as wife as well. 'No, dear Mother, your duty is to your husband. The king, my father is already struck down by grief. He needs you now more than ever. A righteous woman must serve her husband and stay by his side. All our scriptures and wise sages say this' (Ayodhya Kand, Sarga 24).

Kaushalya remained in Ayodhya much against her own wishes. Sadly, her husband, the king, died soon after Rama's departure and she was left alone without husband, son or daughter-in-law. This was her biggest test. She could have turned her anger and sorrow into hatred for Bharat, another son of Dashrath, who was chosen to succeed the king. She could have languished alone in her misery. She could have taken revenge against Dashrath's other queen, Kaikeyi, for banishing Ram.

Kaushalya, instead, became the queen mother. She was no longer just the senior widow of the deceased king, or the mother of the former heir. She urged Bharat to rule instead of forsaking the crown. For fourteen years, she remained the moral guardian and the wise matriarch of Ayodhya. This Ma needed to take on the Rani and Rishika energy to preserve the kingdom and await the return of her son with dignity and hope.

The Ma also grows by getting in touch with her own needs. She has often disowned her Apsara energy in favour of meeting the needs of others. The cultural coding of the Ma and the typical Ma image as an asexual being are so strongly entrenched in our subconscious that many women suppress their vitality and sexuality. They do not realize that this is a result of conditioning rather than their choice. If the Ma cannot own up to her own needs, she becomes dry and dusty. Her service is edged with a quiet desperation. She performs the act of sex as a chore for her partner. She looks after her children, but her heart is not in it. Her children hear the irritation in her voice, they feel her tension. The Ma's guilt at even feeling 'selfish' in this way leads her to overcompensate and micromanage, whether it's her children or her team at work.

The mature Ma is able to channelize her nurturing creative capacity without falling into the traps of guilt and neediness. To do this, she needs to step back and understand which of the other energies are required in her life.

Case Studies

Fatima

Fatima was a participant in a leadership-development programme I conducted for a pharmaceutical company.

A plump jovial woman in her mid-forties, Fatima is the vice president (human resources) at a large pharmaceutical company. She has been in this role for ten years and is very content with her position. Her room is full of pictures of her family, and a large collage of photos of her professional life hangs on a wall. She has the ear of the young CEO and he often consults with her on important decisions. There is something comforting about Fatima that allows the employees to talk freely to her.

She is kind but firm. She has the final say on all matters. Her team members respect her and are also a little scared of getting on her wrong side. She has a great equation with the union leader at their factory in Daman. There have been no major issues with the union in the past few years. 'My legacy is the people I have impacted. Two of my previous team members are CHROs [chief human resources officers] in other companies,' she says with pride.

The recent introduction of a new SAP-and-employee-engagement system globally was a challenging task for Fatima. Technology is not her forte. For a while, she struggled to understand and manage this task. She had always been the one with answers, the one who could be depended upon and the new scenario left her frustrated and confused. She felt that she was letting her team down. She felt that she was not being a good leader and felt guilty that she was not living up to her role. Finally, Fatima had to accept that her younger team members were much more capable than her of handling this project.

She agreed to get some reverse mentoring from the youngest member of her team and delegated the responsibility of implementation to them. 'My kids have grown up,' she admitted to a colleague. She felt a little sad but also proud of her team. She started delegating more work and found the time to undertake the coaching certification course that she had always wanted to do.

Madhavi

Madhavi was one of my first coaching clients who wanted help in achieving a better work-life balance. During our sessions, she shared that she was stressed out at work and felt guilty because she was not being a good mother to her ten-year-old daughter, Natasha. Madhavi had a full-time cook and caretaker at home who took care of her daughter when she came back from school. She mentioned that her husband was very supportive and helped with Natasha's homework. Natasha had never complained about her mother's absence but Madhavi wanted to be there for her daughter, thanks to her own mother having given up her career to take care of Madhavi and her two siblings. Madhavi felt she benefited from the time her mother spent with her, but could not give up her ambitions to be like her. 'I don't want Natasha to tell me later that I was not a good mother. I don't even cook for her like other mothers, or go for the Coffee Morning at her school,' she admitted. Madhavi was a Kanya and a Ma. She wanted to work well and be appreciated for it; she wanted to support her team members and be there for them. She also wanted to be the perfect mother at home. But the guilt was eating away at her. She was also wearing herself out trying to be everything to everyone. When she was with her daughter, she thought about her work and at work she felt guilty because she was not there for Natasha when she returned from school. I gave Madhavi a simple exercise. Every day, she had to write a sentence in her journal: 'I am a good mother because…' Madhavi realized that she was ignoring the many ways in which she supported her daughter and her family. She understood that it was the quality of time and the quality of interactions that she had with her daughter that mattered. When she changed her own mindset about what it meant to be a good mother rather than go with societal expectations of motherhood, she was able to use her Ma energy more effectively and be comfortable in her skin.

9

Rishika: The Wise Seeker

The *Rig Veda* states, 'The entire world of noble people bows to the glory of the glorious woman so that she enlightens us with knowledge and foresight. She is the leader of society and provides knowledge to everyone. She is symbol of prosperity and daughter of brilliance. May we respect her so that she destroys the tendencies of evil and hatred from society' (1.48.8).

The Rishika energy is that of the wise knowledgeable woman. She is the woman that people turn to when they have problems, when they need clarity, when they need spiritual growth and upliftment. The Rishika energy will take the woman on the path of knowledge, whether it is scientific or spiritual. The Rishika woman is an eternal seeker. She longs to know the mysteries of life, death, the universe and god.

The vedas mention twenty-seven women seers who could hold their own with men, among them was Gargi Vachaknavi. She was a great philosopher and expounder of the vedas, who lived in the seventh century BCE. She successfully held her own against a great sage called Yagnavalkya, who was undefeated in intellectual arguments. She wore him down by asking him all kinds of questions about the atman and the soul, till he remarked, 'You ask too much. Ask not too much'—words that have been repeated countless times to curious young girls who have asked too many questions.

He dissuaded her from asking more, as she would lose her mental balance at not being able to comprehend the answers about the true nature of the Brahman! Gargi fortunately was not flustered by this and went on to compose many hymns and become a well-known scholar. She never married.

Another wise woman from this period was Maitreyi, said to be one of the two wives of Yagnavalkya (in many texts she is said to have been a celibate wise woman). When Yagnavalkya said he was drawn to lead the life of an asectic, she wanted to know why. The philosophical dialogue that followed is recorded in the *Brihadaranayka Upanishad*. She is also supposed to have composed ten vedic hymns.

Millennia later came Jahanara Begum, the daughter of Mughal Emperor Shah Jahan. She was the author of the Sufi treatises *Munis-al-Arvah* and *Risala-i-Sahibiyya*. In both works she offers up the spiritual truths as guides and blessings for the reader. She wanted to join the Sufi Chistiya Order but was refused on the grounds of being a woman, and joined the Qadiryya order instead. She wrote, 'When I realized that the truth for this self requires *fanaa* (annihilation of the self), I decided to follow what my pir (master) requires, to die before death, to not wait for death to extinguish me, to become one with the divine.'

Jahanara Begum was respected by her father Shah Jahan and her brothers for her intelligence, piety and diplomacy. Despite being the richest woman of her time with fabulous jewels, buildings and gifts, she described herself as a fakira (poor woman) whose simple tomb was to be covered only by green grass. Jahanara Begum was a Rishika at heart (*Heroines*, Ira Mukhoty).

A wise woman need not always be old, though this is the common association with this archetype. The young Rishika is also drawn to knowledge. Her enquiry could be scientific or spiritual. She is curious, intelligent and usually likes school. She is often seen with her nose in a book or busy researching on her computer. She wants to know about things, how they work, why they exist. A Rishika girl with a Rishika mother is encouraged to study and do well. She is sent for classes and supported to develop her mind.

Others may not be as supportive of the Rishika power. 'What will you accomplish if you study so much?' is a question many aspiring Rishikas have been asked. The logic is that the more the girl studies, the more difficult it will be to find a qualified match for her. After all, she cannot marry a man who is beneath her in status. Unfortunately, many young girls in our country are unable to study due to lack of financial resources and the mindset that girls do not need higher education. Many Rishika girls don't get an opportunity to live their full potential. Some even try to hide their intelligence in order to fit in and be accepted. Many Rishikas are encouraged to behave like Kanyas and keep their opinions to themselves. Those without the Veera energy to desire to rebel may quietly accept this norm, since they too have a need for parental and societal approval.

I remember visiting the home of a relative with two young children. The boy who was about seven was asked to impress the guests with his knowledge. He reeled off the names of many countries and capitals to admiring glances from his parents. He could identify the model of a car from a mile off, they said. They spoke about his excellent marks in Maths and Science. His elder sister was also summoned to say hello. She was a quiet unsmiling girl with a book in her hand, a finger holding the page in place. I could see that she was impatient and wanted to get back to the book.

'Oh, she is always reading something,' her mother said with a despairing look. 'Soon we will have to get her thick spectacles.' They were good people. They probably had no idea that they were discouraging a little Rishika in their home.

The Rishika is not all about academic excellence. She is a good problem-solver and can be counted on to give good advice. She is the girl whom others approach for a rational, practical solution to their problems. She is known for her incisive mind, keen wit and oratorical skills. She loves to participate in debates and quizzes. She is a skilled strategist and can connect the dots and see patterns that others cannot. The Rishika is frustrated if others around her don't get it. Sometimes she feels that she is ahead of the others and wishes they would keep up. Teachers praise her but are also a little wary of her. You never know when she will come up with a question that will stump them. Some Rishikas can turn into insufferable know-it-alls but they are usually well-intentioned, motivated by a desire to share their knowledge rather than, show-off.

The young Rishika is a deeply mature and intuitive child. She is drawn to nature and may be found talking to trees and animals. Her parents worry that she is a little 'off'. She says unexpected things which seem either crazy or very wise. She seems to intuitively pick up on signals from adults and knows what to say and do. A young Rishika is often chided for being silent and withdrawn but she is quite happy in her own world. The sensitive Rishika is an empath connected to something deeper in nature and in people. She creates her own world which is far more interesting and fascinating than the mundane world around her.

Rishika's Cultural Coding

In the Ramayan, Mandodari and Tara symbolized the Rishika energy. 'Mandodari's Lament' is an important part of the Ramayan, portraying her anguish and acceptance of the fate of her husband, Ravan. She is described as a skilled, intelligent woman who endured her husband's obsession with power, his rages and his philandering. It was only Mandodari who saw a side of him that others did not. She discharged her duties as a good wife, mother and chief queen, always thinking of the greater good.

Tara, the wife of Vali, the king of the Vanaras, was a beautiful and accomplished queen. Tara too warned her husband against venturing into the battle with Rama. While Vali was about to rush into a heated battle in response to his younger brother Sugreev's challenge, Tara advised him to cool-off and think logically. She had heard from spies in the forest that Sugreev had become the helpmate of Ram, who was a great soul and a great warrior. She suspected foul play and feared for Vali's life. However, Vali did not listen to her and charged ahead.

Later as he lay dying, he was repentant and realized his wife's great wisdom and intelligence. He gave his younger brother Sugreev this advice, 'Tara is very wise and shrewd, with expertise to analyse and grasp the details of all matters. What she advises you to do will be free from bad consequences. Once she assesses a matter in a particular way, it will not occur otherwise' (Aravamudan, 2014).

Both widows, Tara and Mandodari, married the younger brothers of the men killed by Ram, and remained queens. Whether they lived happily ever after or not was not a matter of interest to the epic writers. Rishikas were not the heroines, they were supporting characters who were usually relegated to minor roles.

Some Rishikas devoted themselves to the spiritual path and became mystics who left the ordinary, 'normal' lives of other women. These were single women who, forsaking family and society, chose a different path. Meerabai, Andal, Avvaiyar, Lalded and Akka Mahadevi are venerated, not just for their spirituality and devotion but for their poetry and writing, which are relevant even today. Their quest was to know and experience the divine. Meerabai and Andal experienced the divine as a lover.

Some Rishikas pursue the divine as a symbol of truth. This deep thirst for knowledge gives them the courage to break away from the herd and follow their own path. However, later myths and stories show that these wise women had to pay a price for their desire for knowledge and freedom, being branded as witches—the 'dayans' who performed black magic and corrupted souls. It did not take much for a wise woman, who was respected as a medicine woman and healer, to be branded a witch if one of her remedies failed.

This continues to happen even in contemporary India. A report from Partners for Law in Development shows that the practice of witch hunting is still prevalent in many parts of the country. One of the findings of the report is that 'Any woman who is exceptional looking, strong-minded, educated or aspires to be educated stands a greater chance of being labelled a witch.'

An article in *India Today* drawn on National Crimes Research Bureau data showed that over 2,000 women were killed in India for practising 'black magic' between 2001 and 2014.

Most of these women were old and alone. Witch hunts are often the result of personal animosity or property disputes, but the notion of the wicked old woman who can cast a spell, or an evil-eye, still persists. There is no organized persecution of male witchdoctors/warlocks/tantriks, but women who have 'magical' powers, who don't fit into the usual moulds are seen with suspicion and fear.

Most narratives, whether from mythology or history, tell us that the price for wisdom was mostly paid by the sacrifice of youth and beauty, or family ties. While the Rishika's energy is often associated with older women, we have lived with the notion that intelligence and the serious quest for knowledge cannot coexist with youth and beauty. Western cultures play out the Dumb Blonde archetype—a beautiful attractive woman who is stupid and frivolous. In India, we believe that wise women cannot be 'normal' in the same way that other women can.

For a long time I believed that women who were wise and intelligent did not wear makeup or pay attention to fripperies like fashion and jewels. There was no room for the Apsara energy if you wanted to be wise and respected by others. The story of Avvaiyar had left deep impression on me. I had seen the movie as a child, in Chennai, and subsequent impressions and stories had somehow firmed the notion that the pursuit of academic excellence or a worthy calling entailed looking serious and respectable. Many people outside of Tamil Nadu may not have heard of Avvaiyar. Here is the popular version of the tale.

Avvaiyar's Story (Tamil Nadu, Fifth Century BCE)

It was the day of her wedding and Avvai had never been more unhappy in her life. Marriage! How she hated that word. It was all her parents talked about after receiving the rich merchant's proposal. He had seen her when she was walking to the river and had fallen in love on the spot. The proposal had been accompanied by a rich sari and gold jewels, which her mother could not stop admiring.

Her parents had long been worried about her marriage, for Avvai had a formidable mind. She knew all the scriptures and composed devotional songs to Lord Vinayaka. Once she had smartly answered a question put by a visiting priest and impressed him with her quick response and knowledge. Her mother, Sivakami, worried how she would manage a kitchen and a household, when she showed no interest in any of the things that other girls of her age enjoyed. How would she get a match who was her equal in looks and intelligence? How would Avvai manage if she didn't? The girl seemed to be in her own world half the time, speaking to herself, writing poems and talking about gods and goodness. The rich merchant was a godsend in Sivakami's eyes.

Avvai's friends envied her, 'You are so lucky,' they said. Not only was Avvai smart, intelligent and beautiful, she was also very fortunate to get such a good match. It seemed as though she had everything, thanks to the blessings of Lord Vinayaka.

Everyone thought her daily prayers to the elephant-headed god had been answered.

But Avvai had a secret. She had never prayed for a good husband and male children like her friends. She had not even prayed for good health and prosperity. She prayed only to learn her purpose. 'Tell me what my purpose is, my lord!' she implored. 'Why have I been put on this earth? What is the destiny I am to fulfil?' She had known all along that she was not meant for the life of a housewife. Over the last few days, she had felt that she was coming closer to this purpose. She had to serve her god by serving the people. How was she going to do it? She had no idea. She only knew marriage would put an end to it.

Now, she could hear the sound of the nadaswaram in the distance announcing the arrival of the wedding party. The heavy gold necklace felt like a noose around her neck, the silver anklets weighed her feet down. Her friends and relatives had rushed out to greet the wedding party, leaving her alone for a few minutes. Avvai stood up. The back door was still unlocked. She slipped out not knowing where she was headed. Her legs seemed to move of their own accord. She walked down the familiar path to the river, to the small temple of Lord Vinayaka where she prayed every day. He had deserted now but she had nowhere else to go.

The idol of the gentle elephant god gazed down at her. Did she sense compassion in his eyes or was it just a mocking smile saying, 'Why are you railing against the fate of every young woman in this land?' The words of her friends rang hollow in her ears. 'He fell in love with your youth and beauty.' This youth and beauty were a burden to her. She didn't want them anymore. Would any suitor be attracted to her if she were old and ugly? Would anyone stop to stare at her if she were not young?

'My lord,' she prayed. 'Take away my youth and beauty. Take away this shape and give me the form of an old woman.' She knew now what she had to do, the path that her life would take unfolded before her with beautiful clarity. 'Please Lord Vinayaka, help me fulfil my life's purpose,' she prayed. She surrendered to the lord.

By the time her parents and the wedding party found her, Avvai had vanished. In her place, stood an old woman with a gentle face and a simple sari. She held a walking stick in her hand. Her eyes twinkled and her smile was kind. 'Goodbye,' she wished them all and left, walking briskly down the road. She had a lot of work to do.

Rishika's Relationships

The Rishika needs to respect the man as an intellectual and spiritual equal before she can love him. She wants stimulating conversation and to be engaged intellectually first. She likes a verbal sparring partner and does not shy away from arguing with him to prove a point. Many Rishika women find partners who have more or similar educational qualifications as theirs. Men are often intimidated by the extroverted Rishikas, thinking that they are 'too brainy and argumentative' or dismiss the introverted ones as being too studious and boring.

As a spouse, the Rishika is loyal and devoted to her partner. Once she has committed, she is in it for better or for worse. She will give her all to make the relationship work, providing wise counsel, solving problems and keeping things organized and functioning smoothly in the household. She is a safe comforting presence to return to, provided her partner does not do stupid things like leaving the toothpaste cap off or lose the dry-cleaning bill.

The Rishika in a relationship will always do the right and proper thing. She is aware of her duties and will not fail them. No one can fault her for anything, but she will not evoke those warm fuzzy feelings either. She knows what gifts to get for her loved ones and plans early for special events. But she is puzzled as to why everyone seems to like her pretty but silly cousin more.

Sometimes, the Rishika can seem distant and disconnected. She may prefer to finish a good book rather than go out with people. It is not that she does not like people; socializing is just not a priority for her. She refrains from posting sentimental posts on Facebook and gushing greetings on WhatsApp. The Rishika has a few good friends. Even though they may not be actively in touch with each other, they connect deeply and can spend a long time in conversations when they meet. She will speak passionately when she is interested in a subject, but small talk is not her cup of tea.

In the Bengali movie *Antaheen* (The Endless Wait; 2018), Aparna Sen plays the character of a strong and intelligent woman who is estranged from her husband even though there is a bond between them. There is no such thing as an ideal relationship, she tells a young women in her office. 'Distance matters,' she almost justifies herself. When her nephew remarks that it is the ego that keeps her and her husband apart, she replies, 'Absence is required to feel a person's presence more intensely.' She prefers to keep a distance rather than admit her vulnerability. Though a talented and articulate woman, she finds it difficult to express her needs and desires and finds some kind of solace in work. She confesses that 'The key to a successful relationship is the ability to compromise,' but her own inability to compromise keeps her removed from a close connection.

Rishika women may be quite contented alone, especially after a certain age. If they have intellectually stimulating pursuits and a passion to devote their time to, they may forego the traditional roles of a housewife and mother. They will pursue a spiritual path and if they choose to have friends, one or two of them need to be soul mates. They do have bouts of loneliness but often the effort needed to form a close relationship does not seem worth it. A cat perhaps?

In most stories from our culture, the Rishika is a celibate woman. Avviayar and Andal were poetesses whose devotion was only to god. Jahanara Begum never married. These women had to forsake (in fact, preferred to give up) worldly attachments in the pursuit of knowledge, spirituality or art. It is difficult to find a great and learned woman who also enjoyed a happy family life and had several children.

Many women reached the Rishika stage later in their lives as wise old grandmothers, who liberally gave advice and imparted knowledge to future generations.

Rishika's Career Choices

Rishikas love to be lifelong learners. Many a Rishika has a doctorate and devotes her life to the study of a subject that she finds fascinating. Rishikas enjoy research and going to the depths of issues that they care about. Good problem-solvers, they look for better ways and new ideas. Many Rishikas tend to prefer Maths and Science since it appeals to their logical brain, yet they are also writers and poets and have a way with words to communicate their ideas to the world. At their best, Rishikas are wise and intelligent women who lead a moral life and make the world a better place. They are calm, incorruptible and can be depended upon to do the right thing.

Rishikas make great teachers, lawyers, scientists, policy-makers and consultants. They can work steadily in the background without wanting the spotlight or recognition. Often, the quality of their work is their own reward. Rishikas often prefer the role of a strategic thinker to the operational doer. They do not like to work in large teams. Even if they adapt to other people, they are still quite happy to work alone or with a few people they know and trust.

Rishikas are also drawn to healing and spirituality. They make great coaches and counsellors, combining a keen insight into the human condition with the desire to contribute their knowledge and learning to others. They may have knowledge of plants, communicate with nature, know the phases of the moon and the whims of the winds. They are the medicine women who hoard arcane knowledge that is lost to others.

Many Rishikas who can tap into their Veera energies can become activists and devote their lives to a cause they believe in. Savitribai Phule and Rokeya Hussain were writers and pioneers of women's education in pre-Independence India. The author Mahashweta Devi fought for the rights of tribals. More recently, Vandana Shiva and Sunita Narain are scholars and researchers who are also environmental activists. When Rishikas use their knowledge for social change, they become a formidable force.

Mature Rishika are renunciates. Once they feel that they are on their chosen path, they are ready to give up all their material possessions. Their deep nature calls for solitude and silence. They transcend the need to be right and righteous and move to a world beyond basic needs, only the quest for truth and meaning remains.

Rishika as a Leader

If given the chance to be a leader, the Rishika will discharge their duties admirably. While they do not actively seek out positions of power, they treat power as a responsibility. They will bring a cool analytical ability to the role and are excellent at long-term thinking and strategy creation. They hold their own when challenged and vigorously defend their position with details and facts. Rishikas make excellent consultants in organizations where they have the opportunity to use their expertise and knowledge. Most people in the organization look to them for answers to business problems.

A compassionate Rishika will provide a shoulder to cry on, but becomes impatient with people who have fuzzy thinking and appear confused and disorganized. In the same vein, the Rishika respects her boss only if he or she is proven to be more knowledgeable and intelligent. He or she has to be someone the Rishika can learn from, someone who will challenge her. An unworthy boss will be met with contempt and she will take matters into her own hands. She will be outraged if you question her integrity or intentions.

The Rishika is a little uncomfortable in the role of team leader. Cool logic does not work with messy human emotions. She prefers to leave people to their own devices after giving them clear instructions and expects them to be as committed and disciplined as she is. She is invariably disappointed when the quality of work does not meet her standards. In such a case she will take over the task. She does not like doing this, but feels she has no choice—no one else has as much expertise as her.

Rishikas gladly attend team meetings and functions out of a sense of duty, but like to keep the personal separate from the professional.

Many Rishikas would rather be the power behind the throne rather than sit on the throne themselves. They usually do not want positional power with its added responsibilities. Instead they prefer the power that comes from deep knowledge and expertise. They are happy to be valued for their sage advice and the knowledge that they are indispensable to the positional leader.

THE EXPERT HISTORIAN—ROMILA THAPAR

There are many historians and academicians but few rise to the top of their chosen field and spend their lives in the study and pursuit of one subject. Romila Thapar, 88, is an expert in ancient Indian history and has authored over fifteen books on the subject. She was a professor at Jawaharlal Nehru University in Delhi and a visiting professor at Cornell, University of Pennysylvania, and College de France. She holds a slew of honorary doctorates form eminent institutions. She has translated her childhood curiosity into her life's work in an area she is clearly passionate about.

Romila Thapar wanted to go to London for higher studies. Her father told her that he had some money but it could either be used for her dowry or to finance her studies abroad. Romila easily chose the latter. She continued to complete her PhD in London and embarked on a distinguished career. She never married.

Like many Rishikas, Romila Thapar did not crave a larger platform outside her work. She refused the Padma Bhushan offered by the Government of India, twice. In a letter to the president, Miss Thapar explained the reason for turning down the award as 'I decided some years ago that I would only accept awards from academic institutions or those associated with my professional work and not accept state awards.'

This lady has been steadfast in sticking to her ideas and beliefs even in the face of many controversies. Thapar's textbooks were published in the late 1960s and quickly sparked controversy. In 1969, members of the Parliamentary Consultative Committee insisted that Thapar's textbook state categorically that Aryans were indigenous to India. She could not find sufficient evidence to support the claim and the demand was ultimately rejected.

https://blogs.loc.gov/kluge/2015/03/who-writes-history/

In the 1970s, officials lobbied for her textbooks to be proscribed. Attacks came again in the late 1990s, as her books were accused of being anti-Hindu and anti-Indian – charges for which she received death threats. Through it all, Thapar argued for the legitimacy of independent historical interpretations based on reliable evidence. She asserted that textbooks should not merely recite cherished myths but provide researched and rational explanations of the past.

Like many Rishikas, she could appear stubborn and arrogant to her critics, believing in the rigour of her scholarship and expertise. In 2019, the Jawaharlal Nehru University asked Miss Thapar to submit her CV since it was examining her status as Professor Emerita. She refused to comply and stated that the Emerita status was a lifelong honour based on past achievements.

In an interview to *The Hindu*, she said, 'They don't recognize that the university is a place where you think freely, where you do research, where you argue and debate ideas.'

In this statement, Romila Thapar echoes the ancient Vedic scholars like Gargi and Maitreyi who thought freely, argued, debated, and did not shy away from expressing their views.

Rishika's Power Sources: Knowledge and Wisdom

The early-stage Rishika accumulates information, the mature Rishika gains wisdom. She is objective and rational in her decision-making. She gets her power from her ability to observe with detachment and speak with clarity.

The Rishika is also an inventor and investigator. She can be relentless in the pursuit of truth and the higher purpose. She also has the power of healing. The Rishika is the custodian of arcane knowledge and she can use this for a good cause. The Rishika in her full power is a woman in full control of her senses, with a higher consciousness and a larger purpose. Her presence is serene, exuding light and love for the whole world.

Rishika's Core Need: Mastery

Along with a deep desire to know and have access to secret knowledge, the Rishika's human need is to be right. This enhances her self-esteem and confidence. She loves the feeling of mastery she gets when she solves something and does something very well. Her self-esteem comes from being able to solve problems and disseminate knowledge. She will argue and argue till the other person admits defeat. She has a great memory and is able to bring up obscure facts read a long time ago, to bolster her arguments.

The Rishika lives by a strong personal moral code. She believes in a righteous life and is extremely principled. She usually sees the world in black and white, and while she is comfortable with the greys, she prefers clarity to ambiguity. She lives with purpose and can be single-minded in the pursuit of a just cause to which she can devote her life.

If torn between what they know is right, and loyalty to loved ones, Rishikas are willing to sacrifice relationships to uphold their most sacred principles. Rishikas become right by acquiring knowledge, often just for the sake of it. They like to be an expert at whatever they do. No half measures for them. Rishikas are absolute in their devotion to the cause or area of study, often sacrificing everything in its pursuit.

Rishika's Power Blocks

Rishika women, like the Kanyas, are most susceptible to the Imposter Syndrome. They are worried that they may not know enough, be smart enough. They often feel that the world does not understand them. They experience inner conflicts between multiple contradictory desires, which may leave them moody and desolate. Some Rishikas in their quest for mastery can also abuse their powers and lose sight of moral imperatives.

Emotionally Drained by: Emotional Frigidity

The Rishika is often so deeply engrossed in the world of intellect or fantasy that she finds it difficult to deal with the real world of messy human emotions. Rishikas react to emotional situations by shutting down and withdrawing. They lock themselves up in their lonely tower, which feels safe and comforting. But they are hurting inside, unable to find a key to unlock their emotions.

Women with an overabundance of Rishika energy, need to express energies from some of the other archetypes as well, otherwise they become frigid in intimate relationships, avoiding sexual and emotional intimacy, wallowing in self-righteous loneliness.

This inability to own and express their emotional needs leads to blocks in their lives. Rishikas can waste away in an arid, dry land of their own making, unable to communicate and connect even with the people they love. They become victims of their own ego, unwilling to come down from the shaky pedestal they have put themselves up on. They can be seen as rigid, unyielding and stubbornly stuck to some principle or reason in their minds.

Their attraction towards the austere and absolute makes them denounce their own emotional needs and feelings. But what they suppress festers and, in the absence of a healthy outlet, it can eat them up from inside. In their extreme shadow, they appear unmoved, cold, thoughtless and cruel to others, insensitive and almost inhuman. The White Witch in the *Chronicles of Narnia*, who froze the land for a hundred years, also has a frozen heart (Lewis, 2010).

Fears: Exposure and Criticism

The Rishika does not like to be proven wrong. She has spent her whole life working hard and upholding certain principles. She has taken such pains to be thorough and flawless. She does not mind criticism of her looks or behaviour but she feels great pain if anyone criticizes the quality of her work or doubts her intentions and intelligence.

The Rishika girl is in constant fear of being seen as stupid or ignorant. She will never raise her hand in class if she is not 100 per cent sure of the answer. She will never commit if she is not 100 per cent sure of her ability to deliver. She is afraid that something will go wrong and she will be exposed as incompetent and useless. The Rishika takes calculated risks if she is clear about her purpose and principles. It is this fear that makes the Rishika seem rigid and inflexible. She is just not yet completely sure about making the change. She needs more proof that this project will work.

Responds with: Withdrawal or Arrogance

The Rishika is in danger of being caught in this circle of anxiety and fear. Her desire to avoid exposure and criticism can make her paranoid, distant and fastidious. This hampers her productivity and passion and she obviously does not get the results she wants. This makes her even more unhappy, pessimistic and fearful. She then adopts a protective strategy and hides away alone in her ivory tower, escaping into her comfort zone. She is willing to stay there for as long as it takes.

Other Rishikas become arrogant and abuse their power of knowledge. In order to protect their identity, they use sarcasm or humiliation to belittle others who are not as 'intelligent' as them. They try to prove their superiority by assuming a ' know it all' attitude which alienates other people. When questioned, they will retaliate with glib responses and obfuscation, never accepting that they could be wrong!

How the Rishika Grows

The Rishika can grow only if she comes out of her ivory tower into the messy real world. She needs to connect with her own emotions and the emotions of others. She needs to stop looking at people as problems to solve, and must learn to empathize. The Rishika will be tested in a situation that calls for real human connection. She usually avoids funerals and weddings, since she is not comfortable with open and public display of emotions. The Rishika has emotions, she just does not express them freely and frequently.

She needs to let others into her circle of trust and have relationships where she can be vulnerable. Sometimes, being vulnerable just means saying 'I don't know' or 'I made a mistake'. Sometimes, it means confessing your love to a person without being sure of their response. It means risking emotional exposure. The Rishika is quite willing to take calculated risks and will be well-prepared for any eventuality.

But she is at a loss when it comes to unpredictable people. Being more open and honest in relationships helps her to meet her need for connection and love, which she may sacrifice in favour of being right. Asking for forgiveness is another expression of vulnerability and courage for the Rishika.

It is often mistakenly assumed that older women are inherent Rishikas who have no need of material pleasures or desires. Just as youth and beauty are seen as enemies of wisdom and gravitas, age seems to have connotations of celibacy and abstinence for women in our culture. In the movie *Badhai Ho* (Congratulations, 2018), an older woman, Mrs Kaushik, becomes pregnant at a much later stage in life. This news shocks her two children, horrifies her relatives and makes her feel embarrassed. The cultural coding is clear. After a certain stage, even marital sex is seen as unnatural for women. While her husband preens in the affirmation of his masculinity, the wife squirms with shame. Spiritual pursuits are supposed to replace sexual pleasures once a woman reaches a certain age.

This may come easily and naturally to some Rishikas, but it does not mean that all older women automatically have the Rishika energy. There is suppressed Apsara energy in many older women, seeking expression and release. The Rishika needs to recognize and express this energy as well to be emotionally and sexually fulfilled.

The Rishika has to let a bit of imperfection into her world and be secure in the knowledge that she can handle it. She needs to face the reality of not knowing, of messiness and ignorance.

In the film *Yeh Jawaani, Hai Deewani* (The Madness of Youth; 2013) the heroine, Naina, is a serious, shy, introverted Rishika who prefers to study and pursue her passion. She is a topper in class and is quite content with the sober pace of her life until a chance encounter with Aditi, her school friend, triggers change. Naina does something completely atypical, she takes a spontaneous trip by herself to the hills, and an adventure begins. She is fearful of exposure and yet longs for new experiences. During a game on a train, Naina feels that she has been missing out on the 'real' experiences of life. Bunny, another former classmate and a fellow traveller, shows Naina that she too has a 'cool' side, though Naina herself feels that she is boring. Towards the end of the trip, Naina falls in love with Bunny but is unable to express her feelings to him. Naina is able to move on and accept her life. Eight years later, as a more mature Rishika, she is able to declare her love for Bunny while retaining her pragmatic Rishika energy.

In my early days as a facilitator, I would be quite anxious about the outcome of the workshops. I would prepare well, send details of logistics well in advance, come an hour early before sessions so that nothing would go wrong. While nothing went wrong, I later realized that I was not in my flow in the sessions. I would have some anxiety that I was not going to be on time, I would not cover the content, that I would not satisfy the participants, that the feedback would not be perfect, etc.

After I started doing the work of personal transformation and leadership, I received feedback from my colleagues that I came across as 'intellectual' and 'correct' and 'distant'. After doing my own inner work, connecting to my purpose, I have found more joy and ease in my work. I still plan and prepare because as a Rishika, my need to be right, to be the expert has not disappeared. But I have become more comfortable talking about my vulnerabilities, going with the flow and more secure in my expertise.

The Rishika leader is well respected for her knowledge and insights, but she cannot depend only on that for her growth. Sometimes, she may not have all the answers so she will need to delegate and get others to do things. She needs to get out of her cubicle and engage more with people around her. She needs to learn storytelling skills instead of relying only on facts and data to influence and get alignment from others. The Rishika leader assumes that her logical analysis will automatically get a buy-in, and she ignores the other aspects of human emotions and needs. The Rishika can be direct and blunt without realizing the emotional state of the other person. She will benefit from emotional-intelligence training to enhance her interpersonal sensitivity.

If the Rishika taps into the optimism and charm of the Kanya, the nurturing empathy of the Ma, and the fearless risk-taking ability of the Rani, she can become a respected and excellent leader.

Case Studies

Paromita

Paromita was one of my coaching clients.

Paromita had a PhD in Econometrics from a reputed American university. She had published several papers and was one of the youngest professors in her field. She received an offer from a consulting firm to join their analytics division as a senior researcher. She would receive three times what she made as a professor. Paromita had not made tenure in her college, so she decided to take up the offer and move to the corporate world.

In the beginning she was excited about her job. She wanted to develop innovative models and work on 'cutting edge' areas of research. But she soon felt that she was not making any headway. She had to manage a team of three junior researchers as well, and she did not see this as part of her job. There were endless rounds of meetings to get approvals. Her colleagues did not seem to understand her. Her team members complained that they did not get feedback or any mentoring from her. Paromita felt that she was an expert in her field and her knowledge was not valued in the organization.

At the end of the year, she received feedback from other employees. She was shocked at some of the scores and comments. Her colleagues perceived her to be: arrogant, distant, pedantic, and out of touch with reality. Paromita, the Rishika, did not come out of her ivory tower and connect with others or understand the needs of other people.

After some coaching with me, Paromita realized that she needed to adapt her communication style to the needs of her audience. She had to translate her knowledge into a language that others would understand. She could not just let her team members work independently on separate projects, but had to get them to collaborate as a team. If she was to succeed in the job, she would have to make changes.

It took her some time, but Paromita started accessing her Kanya power. She became more light-hearted, flexible and in-tune with other people's needs while communicating. She realized that it was possible to be liked by her team and respected for her knowledge.

Sumathy

I came to know about Sumathy's story during a mentoring programme I manage for college students.

Sumathy was a brilliant student who had been a topper all her life. She was a Rishika, an introvert who was most comfortable with her work, her books and studies. She came from a modest lower-middle-class family and lived in a small town in Tamil Nadu. She knew that education was a way for her to succeed and support her family. She had a natural flair for academics, especially Biology and Chemistry and dreamt of becoming a doctor. She was pampered by her teachers who encouraged her to do well. Her classmates were in awe of her. She aced the Class XII board exams and also cleared the medical entrance exams with a rank that gave her admission to a prestigious institution out of the state. She received a scholarship to pursue her dreams. Everyone in her town was extremely proud of her and Sumathy was determined to shine.

Sumathy's problems began when reached college and realized she was not prepared for college life. Hostel life entailed living with others in close quarters. She faced a language barrier with her rusty English and perfunctory Hindi. She found it difficult to meet new people and make friends. She realized that other students were just as smart or even more intelligent than she was, and were confident to boot. She was scared to put her hand up in class for fear of ridicule. The professors were impersonal and very different from her caring teachers in school.

The biggest shock was when she did not get the top marks in her first assignment. She wondered if this was the right career path for her. Yet, she could not let down her family and her teachers back home. She did not want to share her struggles with anyone else. She had always been the smart, capable one and she could not face the fact that she was just another average student. She did what most Rishikas do when faced with challenges—she shut down and withdrew into herself.

Fortunately for Sumathy, she met a professor who was also from Tamil Nadu. This doctor had gone through the struggles that Sumathy was facing and took Sumathy under her wing. Under Dr Lata's mentoring, Sumathy slowly opened up. She realized that she needed to take on this challenge and tap into her Veera energy. This was very different from an academic challenge that she could handle. Dr Lata introduced Sumathy to a couple of senior students who helped Sumathy with spoken English tuitions.

Soon Sumathy started asking questions in class. She slowly started coming out of her shell. She overcame her fear and started attending social events. By the end of the first year, Sumathy had made a couple of friends, girls like her from small towns who felt lost and out of place in the college. As her confidence returned, Sumathy started to do better in her studies as well.

10

The Journey to Becoming Powerful

The journey to power is not about grabbing power along the way, or making it to the list of the 'Ten Most Powerful Women in the World'. It is not about toppling men from their pedestals or taking their place. It is not about being a badass or kick-ass or a she-devil. There is a difference between being in a position of power and feeling powerful. Becoming powerful is about a personal transformation that makes the most of your unlimited personal resources.

All of us have experienced those highs in our lives when we are in the flow, completely in the moment, experiencing joy and connection. We feel invincible, we feel we can do anything. There are no blocks to our power. We are doing exactly what we are meant to in this universe. This is power.

The transformations thrust upon women—menstruation, marriage, motherhood, menopause—are all life-changing events and each comes with its emotional side-effects. Some women adapt easily, some struggle through it, and some are unable to make some or most of the transitions.

Sometimes, a specific action is needed in a specific situation. Durga, the goddess who was created to destroy the demon Mahishasura, had to vanquish several other demons along the way. Each demon represented a quality or bad habit that we need to get rid of. Durga had a vast array of divine weapons and she used them strategically against her foes and vanquished them all. We can invoke the power archetypes to overcome the demons we face.

- When a Kanya needs to have a courageous conversation with her boss, she can summon all her courage and prepare diligently for that situation. She can succeed, but it will still not be a normal or natural situation for her.
- An Apsara can decide to become disciplined and finish that art project that she has been postponing for a long time. But she could still be erratic and disorganized in many other areas of her life even if she wants to change.
- An introverted Rishika can down several glasses of wine, summon up all her energy and throw a lavish party for fifty people, but she still feels like crawling back to her cave after that.

Becoming powerful is a choice. It is not just about managing one situation alone, it is a journey to becoming the best whole version of ourselves.

It is not easy to change habits that have been cultivated over many years, in some cases a habit that has become such a part of us that it cannot be amputated without pain. This old habit is our identity. This is who we are. It can be quite scary to send that person out and invite a stranger in. But that old version of you, though dear and familiar, is not helping you in the new situation that you have to manage. It is like letting go of a favourite childhood toy or that worn-out blanket that gave you comfort and security. You know you have to leave it behind as you step into adulthood, but you have nothing to replace it.

This journey of transformation is the Hero's journey. We shall assume the Hero includes the Heroine as well. The writer Joseph Campbell was the first to speak about this idea in 1949, but the notion has been around for a long time in classical stories across cultures. From Greek myths to modern Bollywood movies, every story has an element of the Hero's (or Heroine's) journey. As per Campbell, there are three parts to the story.

- The Departure Act: the Hero leaves the Ordinary World.
- The Initiation Act: the Hero ventures into unknown territory (the 'Special World') and is birthed into a true champion through various trials and challenges.
- The Return Act: The Hero returns in triumph.

This was later expanded to include twelve parts, where the protagonist undergoes inner and outer transformation.

The Heroine can be quite happy and comfortable in the ordinary world, until the call comes. She usually refuses the call the first time, until she feels sure that this is the journey she needs to undertake. Most people feel that there is nothing wrong with them. They don't really need to change anything. Life is going along quite well. That is fine too. Maybe it is not the time. Maybe they are just too scared to venture into the unknown. Sometimes, the call is so loud and so urgent that it cannot be ignored.

The movie *Queen* is a classic Heroine's journey. It has been discussed above in the context of the Kanya. The lead played by Kangana Ranaut is a simple middle-class girl called Rani, who is looking forward to her wedding with a man she loves, a man that her parents approve of. She is especially looking forward to the honeymoon abroad. Her world is shattered when her fiancé calls off the wedding. Rani must now choose what she wants to do. Her journey begins when she sets-off alone for her honeymoon to Paris. This is not just a fun trip abroad. Rani is alone, friendless and recovering from a broken heart. This is an act of courage as she shifts from the Kanya to the Veera power.

In the Hindi film *Thappad* (Slap; 2020), the heroine Amrita is slapped, which causes her to re-examine her whole life. She can never go back to being the person she was before that night when her husband slapped her in front of their guests. Life as she knows it starts to unravel and Amrita has to make some tough choices and stand up for herself. She had been happy as a Kanya, and then as the Rani of her little household. She had a steady routine and a companion she loved. After that slap, Amrita has to invoke all her *Veera* energy to brave the world and stand up for what she believes in.

In *Jab We Met* (When We Met; 2007), Geet is the spirited, reckless Veera who runs away from home to be with her lover. She is outspoken, brave and wears her heart on her sleeve without regard for other people's feelings and needs. Her journey of transformation is a move to becoming a more mature and wiser Rishika, who understands the meaning of true love.

The call to transformation does not always come with a crisis, many women opt for the journey of their own volition. The call to serve a greater purpose or pursue a dream is also an opportunity to start the journey towards becoming more powerful. In the Tamil film *Kanaa* (The Dream; 2018), a young village girl called Kowsi starts playing cricket to make her father happy. Her journey is sparked by her dream to win a cricket match.

In the Hindi film *Tumhari Sulu* (Your Sulu; 2017), Sulu is a happy-go-lucky housewife, a true Ma and Rani who becomes a radio jockey, triggering a chain of events in her life. Her role as a mother and wife is tested by her new-found independence and recognition. Her transformation lies in successfully integrating all her powers, without sacrificing her values.

I use this construct in the workshops I conduct for women. In one of these sesisons, the *Write Your Life* workshop, the participants spoke about the heroine's journey in their lives—for one it was marriage, for another, an overseas assignment in a foreign land, for another woman, it was leaving the small town she grew up in for the big city to pursue her studies.

The Heroine has to face many conflicts and trials before she reaches her goal. She will need to battle her inner demons, as well as outer challenges. She needs to confront her shadows, see that part of her that she has kept locked away. She will be forced to accept her dark side and then come to accept and own it. It is in doing this that her true transformation begins. She realizes her power is not something that someone else bestows on her. In fact, the Heroine is at her lowest point when she realizes her power, a time when something that she always had within her needs to be awakened.

In the Hindi movie *Queen*, the heroine realizes this when she is confronted by a thief but struggles, fights and manages to hold on to her handbag. This victory gives her the confidence to go on. The path to wholeness is filled with successes and defeats. The Heroine has to move on, without distractions, without being swayed by a win or disillusioned by a loss.

In the Hindi film *Panga* (Clash; 2020), Jaya is a national-level kabaddi player, a Veera who loves the game and is determined to make a success of her career. However, the sight of her vulnerable premature baby awakens the Ma in her, and she subdues her Veera power. Yet, though she is content, she is not completely happy. She has not moved to wholeness because the repressed Veera yearns for liberation.

Jaya's transformation happens when she is able to reconcile the Ma and the Veera in her. This involves actively giving up the Ma role and reconciling to the fact the she has to leave her husband and son to fend for themselves when she goes for training. The move to wholeness is not easy. It involves a paradigm shift in our worldview. Jaya has to confront not only her own bias, but that of a patriarchal norm—mothers who pursue their own dreams are selfish; a woman's first responsibility is to her family.

Becoming powerful is a journey of transformation. For women who have been denied power, or even for those who have voluntarily forsaken power, it can be a scary journey. All the case studies you have read in the previous chapters are stories of real women who changed something about themselves to become happier and more fulfilled.

I often quote Marianne Williamson from *Reflections in Love*, in my workshops with women: 'Our deepest fear is not that we are inadequate. Our deepest fear is that we are powerful beyond measure. It is our light, not our darkness that most frightens us' (Williamson, 1992).

Embarking on the journey to becoming powerful does not mean that we have to accomplish extraordinary things, though some women have done that. It is not an adventure sport that plays out in the external world. It does not culminate in a standing ovation from an audience. This journey is about acknowledging our authentic power. Sometimes, this can be scary as well. Sometimes, we have become so reconciled to lives of quiet desperation in a cocoon of denial that it is difficult to imagine an alternate life. Many of us are still in love with a story that no longer serves us. Rewriting that story is an act of courage and requires effort and dedication.

As long as I believe that conflicts are bad and are to be avoided at all costs, I remain safe from conflicts. I can easily intellectualize my belief as a rational action in a world of unnecessary violence. However, I know that it is only by speaking my mind and risking conflict that I will truly grow.

The transformational journey to becoming powerful can be dangerous if undertaken alone. On her journey, the Heroine always meets a mentor or guide who shows her the way. This can be a friend, an older person, a coach, a boss or even a guiding energy. In the Hollywood epic blockbuster *Star Wars* (1977), Luke had a mentor in Obi Wan Kenobi, the Jedi knight. In the *Lord of the Rings* trilogy (2001, 2002, and 2003), Frodo had Gandalf and his friend Sam to help him on the journey. Many successful career women have spoken about the mentors and guides who have helped them on the journey to leadership. Indra Nooyi credits a large part of her success to the good mentoring and coaching she received from her mentors.

A mentor could be a parent like Mahavir Phogat, the wrestler who coached his daughters to become champion wrestlers. A mentor can come in the form of a friend who is there for the journey. In the movie *Panga*, Jaya—a mother who wants to make a comeback as a kabaddi player—turns to her friend Meenu for support, encouragement and guidance.

Sometimes, a guide can be a book, like the Bible or the Gita or Quran.

The six archetypes—Kanya, Apsara, Veera, Rani, Ma, and Rishika—are also guides for the journey to becoming powerful. Knowing about the powers innate in us and understanding the powers represented by the other archetypes is important. Imagine you are going to a strange new land. It helps if you have a map, have some understanding of the language and some tools to navigate the new territory. Instead of blundering in this new land and learning only by trial and error, you now have something valuable to help you. All heroes have received help in some form or the other on the journey.

So, how can you use the knowledge of the six power archetypes as a guide; how can you use it to manage some of the struggles that you face on a daily basis, or navigate a crisis? You can do so by ensuring the following.

Know Yourself

First, do read about all six archetypes. As you read, connect to your own experiences and beliefs. Which power do you most resonate with? Which sentences have you nodding or thinking, 'This is so like me!'

Identify one or two dominant archetypes that you recognize are within you. You can also take the 'PowerfuLife Assessment' on the website www.powerfulife.in. This is a validated tool that has been developed using the Six Feminine Powers Model. It will give you a clear idea about your Power Profile. Remember, any assessment tool is as good as your own assessment of yourself. If you are not sure, ask a few people who know you really well. Check with your boss, your spouse, your best friend. They will corroborate (or contradict!) your own assessment.

Identify Current Goals and Context

Just because you have a nice new hammer, it doesn't mean you have to find some shiny nails to bash in. Maybe your dominant powers are working very well for you now. Maybe you are not ready for the journey of transformation. It is possible that you want to make only a couple of changes that you knew all along were needed to your behaviours. Maybe, you are living your dream now.

Well, good luck to you. The Six Feminine Powers Model can be a useful resource for you, if you need them in the future. Chances are that you will. Life usually throws up situations that are important for our growth. If you do face any, come back to this book and use them. If not, identify your goals:

- What are the big dreams you have now, at this stage of your life?
- If you don't have a big dream, is there some nagging issue, a challenging situation or something you want to get better at?
- Do you want to find a partner, but are just not able to make a commitment?

- Do you want to quit your job and become an entrepreneur?
- Do you want to have a better relationship with someone close to you?
- Do you want to run away from home and become an actress?
- Do you want to buy a home for your parents?

Usually, we are chasing some dream or the other.

My dream was to write a book that would help thousands of women in India and enable them to be happy, fulfilled and successful. For a long time, it was just a dream. I wrote several articles, I set up a company to train and coach women, but still had not come up with something unique that could be made into a book.

Write down your goals and dreams, if you are serious about them.

Complete the sentence, 'My life would be great, if only—'

Transformation and changes happen in a context. The context could be getting stuck when you are solving a problem or failing repeatedly when pursuing a goal. Change takes effort and has to be worth it. Of course, the world thrusts change on us as well. During the Corona pandemic, many people had change forced upon them. All of us needed to adapt to survive. Some did it well, some struggled. Almost everyone had to change.

Determine the Change You Need to Make

Once you determine the change you need to make, you can determine the power you need in that context. You can identify the power block you are facing that is creating the challenging situation.

In my case, I was dithering over my dream of a book. I had a huge period of inaction followed by bouts of self-doubt. My Rishika power enabled me to come up with the idea and do the research. But my power was blocked by my Kanya, who has a fear of rejection. Ironical as it may seem, I kept dragging my feet on completing the book proposal, since once I sent it out it could mean a rejection from a publisher. This, despite the fact that I had written two books!

I had to overcome that hesitation and become more disciplined and relentless. I needed to awaken my Veera in this context.

Based on the knowledge of the Six Feminine Powers, you can identify the powers needed for you to overcome the challenge or achieve your goal. This could be your shadow power. The one quality that you find annoying or irritating in others could be what you need to develop in you.

Case Studies

Savita

Savita attended one of the retreats that I facilitated.

Savita, a Veera in a financial-services company, was tired of all the years of hard work she had put in. She was getting no joy from her role as senior vice president. She had turned fifty-two, and felt a need to slow down and focus on other things. She was longing to harness her Rishika, which had lain dormant for so long. Yet, her identity was so closely connected to her job, that she also hesitated to lose that achieving and ambitious part of her.

Savita took the step of resigning her job with no particular plan in mind. She wanted to help other women, write a book of poetry, and go for a Vipassana retreat and spend time connecting with herself. She had not lost her Veera power, but now used it to meet the needs of the Rishika in her.

Shafia

Shafia works in the human resources department with a large organization for whom I do leadership-development work. Shafia, a dominant Apsara, had become a caregiver to her elderly parents. Her only sibling, her younger brother, was studying in Australia. Her father had suffered a stroke and her mother had chronic arthritis. They managed by themselves in Indore with some help from two maids. During the lockdown imposed by the Corona pandemic, Shafia had taken a transfer to be able to live with her parents, since external help was not available. She now worked from home and tried to juggle her office work and caregiving activities.

Initially, she felt resentful toward her brother for what she perceived as his abandoning the parents. She was annoyed that she had to give up her happy-go-lucky single-woman lifestyle in the city, to move back to her childhood home. Shafia realized that her attitude was not helping her or her parents. She needed to invoke the caring, nurturing, empathetic Ma power to make peace with the choices she had made.

Invoke Your Power

Once you decide the power archetype you need to harness or invoke, it is important to implement the actions to do so. While just the realization is enough for some to make a conscious shift, for others, specific, focused actions are needed. Some people will have quick breakthroughs, others will face failure and require years of practice to learn what they need to learn. If the power is your shadow, then you will first need to come to terms with this aspect before you can actively invoke the power.

The next chapter will provide you with the practices to harness and invoke the powers that you need in your life and take an appropriate action.

11
Practices to Invoke Your Power

The journey is not easy for the Heroine. Before she embarks on a long journey, she needs to pack her bags well. She needs some food and nourishment, appropriate clothes, a map and a travel kit. Similarly, on the transformative journey to becoming powerful, we need to prepare ourselves well.

This is where sustaining practices are needed. Many of these are common sense, things we may already know—but common sense is not common practice. Women know this best. You can't lose weight by dieting for a day. You can't get those toned abs by working out for just a week. You can't ace the exam by studying just the night before.

We need practices that we can implement regularly. We need to make shifts in our body, in our thinking and in daily actions. There is a strong connection between the body and mind and our spirit. We can access any of these through the other.

The Body

I have been a yoga practitioner for many years and have seen the impact of yogasanas not just on the body, but also on the mind. The combination of a posture, breath and mindfulness leads to better physical and mental health. Yogis know about the nature of the body's chakras or energy centres. When these chakras are activated and open, there is great power that flows through our body. Through this power, we reach the ultimate goal of self-realization.

I learnt from many yoga teachers. My friend and yoga guru Sindu Sanjith has shared many of the specific asanas that help to release chakra energy, and also connect to the power archetype we want to realize. The Ajna chakra or the centre of intuition and self-realization is the place to start, before proceeding to other chakras. This enables a mindful and intentional practice. While most asanas impact several chakras at one time, some are more relevant for our body practices to invoke a particular energy.

When we work on the body, we build muscle memory. Some of us have learnt to ride a cycle in our childhood. Though we may not have touched a bike in twenty years, somehow when we get on one, it all comes back. Similarly a habit built through repetitive practice becomes such a part of us, that unlearning it is a real challenge. I had been so used to driving with manual gears for more than twenty years that it was difficult to learn to drive a car with automatic transmission, even though it was supposed to be much easier to drive!

A Veera's body language is different from the Ma, a Veera needs more flexibility and a Ma needs more strength; a Rishika needs to loosen up and an Apsara needs to develop gravitas.

The subtle changes in the body become a way to develop a more powerful presence. We need to create new patterns, a new posture that allows for a new power to come into being.

The Mind

Our mindsets and thoughts are habits. Our identity has become frozen in time. Our beliefs have become life sentences, since we hold them to be true. A Kanya lives with the belief that only good girls get acceptance. A Veera feels that life is a constant battle. A Rishika has always believed that she can't be beautiful *and* intelligent. The Ma feels that it is a universal truth that people need to sacrifice for others to belong to the group. Some of these beliefs need rewiring, for good. This cannot be a temporary switch.

Psychologists, coaches and therapists support people as they shift fundamental beliefs that hamper their growth. Cognitive Behavioural Therapists (CBT) help clients to identify and shift unwanted negative thought patterns about the self and the world. I work as a life coach who is also accredited in CBT. Through the process of coaching, I help my clients identify certain beliefs that don't help them and enable the shift. This takes patience, time and openness from the clients.

Another way to shift mindsets and thoughts is through positive affirmations.

Affirmations help to reinforce new beliefs and messages about the self. These needed to be repeated like a mantra. Affirmations describe a goal in its completed state. Louise Hay, the author of many books on healing says, 'You have the power to heal your life, and you need to know that. We think so often that we are helpless, but we're not. We always have the power of our minds ... Claim and consciously use your power' (Hay, 1999).

Affirmations help in reframing the way we look at ourselves and manifest the power we want to invoke. Affirmations don't deny your current challenge or reality nor do they tell you to fake it till you make it. They send a message to your subconscious mind and open the door for a new way of being.

Here are some steps to form and use effective affirmations.

- You need to believe in the goal and want it for yourself. Just repeating words without intention is not going to work. Feel the words and believe in them.
- Think about who you need to be to achieve the goal.
- Use positive words in your affirmation: 'I am healthy', instead of 'I am not sick'. 'I am strong', instead of 'I am not weak'.
- Say affirmations in the present tense: 'I am', rather than 'I will'.
- Say these affirmations regularly. Daily. Repeat them.

Rhoda Byrne in her bestselling book *The Secret* also reinforces the power of our thoughts. The Law of Attraction also states that we attract whatever we think of into our lives. Our thoughts and beliefs become the source of our true power. She says, 'The power within you is greater than the power within the world' (Byrne, 2006).

In a way, affirmations are similar to prayers. Most people have prayed at some point of time in their lives to their gods or goddesses asking for material things, or for goals to be achieved. Prayers are intended and involve a certain energy.

Lord Ganesha, for instance gives us the energy to overcome obstacles. Goddess Saraswati gives us knowledge to pass exams. Many people in South India pray to Moodevi, the goddess who helps avert misfortune. Affirmations seek to awaken the goddess within ourselves and invoke the aspect of our power that is most needed.

I am now working with the affirmation, 'I am beautiful and powerful', because I want to invoke more of my Apsara and Veera energy. I have been doing this for the past few months and am seeing shifts in the way I see myself.

The Body, Mind and Heart Together

Apart from working on the body and thoughts, we also can perform certain specific actions that call for a different kind of energy from us. These actions practiced over a period of time become new behaviours that we are comfortable with. The actions can be hobbies that we can cultivate over a period of time or specific actions that we need to take on a daily basis.

I want to be more self-expressive both in my personal and professional life. My Rishika power ensures that I come across as knowledgeable and smart, but sometimes I miss a personal connection. I now make it a point to give a personal example as well, for any concept that I am presenting. I have become more comfortable sharing stories that show my vulnerability. I find that this helps my audience connect with me. The more I started doing this, the more I began to receive feedback that I was 'inspirational' and 'a good motivational speaker'. I do not need to have this in the same degree as a core Apsara, but I can be more expressive about my needs and feelings than I was before.

Someone else can have a different Apsara practice. My friend Diya who was always a tomboy, wanted to invoke her Apsara. She wanted a better relationship with herself and her partner. She started to take better care of herself. This included a new flattering hairstyle, putting on makeup and more feminine clothes that accentuated her curves. This made her feel more in touch with her feminine self, less self-conscious about her looks. She was able to think of herself as attractive. She also took belly dancing lessons. The sensuous movements were different and difficult but soon she took to it like a fish to water. She mentioned that she affirmed 'I am a beautiful woman' every time she looked in the mirror.

To have a long-lasting shift and to experience the powers that we want in our lives, we need to work on all three—Body, Affirmations and Actions.

Practices to Gain Kanya Power

The Kanya power gives us the ability to find joy, peace and relaxation in a busy world. It is the move to innocence and purity from a relentless pursuit of ambition. The Kanya embodies lightness, flexibility and adaptability.

Body Practices

The Kanya walks like a young girl. Sometimes, she seems gawky, sometimes she trips along lightly. Her pace is measured, but not always consistent.

Choose a body practice that is fun, involves movement and dance. Bollywood dancing, or Salsa that is not rigorous or strenuous, is ideal for the Kanya energy to flow freely. A great way to lighten up and loosen up is to put on your favourite music and do free-flow dancing that involves simple flexible movements. The moment a dance form becomes rigorous, structured and competitive, the Kanya energy is lost.

A senior leader I know is a typical Veera-Rani. She loves to go clubbing with her girlfriends, drink lots of wine and dance to retro music. This brings out the lighter, cheerful side, the Kanya, of her personality. While this is not done as a conscious serious practice, she sees this as a ritual that is necessary for her to maintain balance and sanity. This allows her to explore the happy-go-lucky child part of her identity in a safe space.

Yogasanas

The Kanya energy is about returning to innocence, in some ways about starting from the beginning with openness and freshness. The practice needs to build flexibility and humility. You can just stand and bend down to touch your toes, reaching wherever you can and staying there for a few breaths.

Focus on the ajna chakra, or the third-eye chakra, to connect to your pure intuition and innocence. You can do the child's pose or balasana, the puppy pose or the dolphin pose. Asanas that have a forward bend also help to invoke the Kanya power.

Balance these with the counter poses that open the heart chakra or anahata chakra. This balances the opening of the innocent heart with the opening of the conscious mind.

Actions

The actions to invoke the Kanya are playful unstructured activities that allows for spontaneity and lightness. Playing with young children, childhood games like hide-and-seek which do not require intellectual stimulation or a dash to the finish line are ideal actions to invoke the Kanya.

NETHRA'S STORY

One of my coaching clients, Nethra, was a very structured Rani whose children were rebelling against her controlling nature. Even her downtime activities with her children were structured. She had a bedtime routine which never varied—a short quiz followed by a meaningful story with a moral. In her mind, she was doing everything right to give her children a solid foundation for their success. Nevertheless, she was frustrated by not gaining the kind of connection that she wanted, nor getting things done her way.

During our coaching sessions, she realized that her children would not have many happy memories of their childhood. She started doing art with her children, allowing them to paint whatever they wanted and making a bit of a mess. She needed to connect with her own Kanya to be able to do this, without giving instructions. Soon, she and her two daughters started having more fun. She allowed them to choose a bedtime story every alternate day. She was still a structured disciplined mother but now she had more freedom and flexibility.

Just as Nethra, a Rani, learnt how to connect with her Kanya, even Veeras can invoke their Kanya power by just letting go and taking some rest. Getting a good massage to ease the strain and intentionally engaging in self-care will help the harried Veera find some ease. Letting go of a couple of non-critical tasks on her 'to-do' list, in favour of something silly and frivolous is something the relentless Veera needs to do from time to time.

Any action that connects to your own goodness and makes you feel virtuous also helps to connect to the Kanya energy. Any good deed helps. This can be a compliment to a friend, cleaning out your own closet, an act of kindness for your neighbour, forgiving a mistake by the other driver. An act that just helps you achieve your own goal will not help.

Affirmations

The following affirmations can be practiced by a Kanya to become free of her power blocks, and by those who want to invoke their Kanya power as well. The affirmations help to overcome the emotional drain and fears of the Kanya and harness the true Kanya power.

I am good enough.
I am honest.
I am truthful.
I am joy.
I am light.
I am full of hope.
The world is a good and pleasant place.
The world will nurture and support me.
I am pure of heart.
I am loved and accepted for who I am.

Practices to Gain Apsara Power

The Apsara power allows for full free-flowing self-expression and connection with our sexual energy. This is a valuable power for women but many women are clueless about the very existence of this power within them. There is so much cultural shaming around the Apsara that conscious practices are needed to invoke and connect to this power.

Natural Apsaras do this effortlessly, others need to learn.

Body Practices

You notice the Apsara just by her walk. She sways her hips just a bit and moves with grace and sensuality. This is the walk of the woman who knows she is attractive and is aware that people are looking at her. The first body practice is to notice your walk. Allow yourself to flow.

Choose a sensual dance, the kind you would never have dreamt of even seeing. Have fun with it by yourself. I spoke about my friend Diya who took lessons in belly dancing. Belly dancing—which involves moving the pelvic region, the seat of femininity—is a great way to connect to our sensuous core. The Tango and Bachata are other sensuous dances. There are many dance studios and classes in Indian cities that offer these classes. Odissi and Mohiniattam are also emotive sensual dances that are safely traditional as well. Or you can always put on your favourite Indian filmi number and dance in your bedroom.

Another option is pole dancing. I recently saw a film on Aarifa Binderwala who is an expert pole dancer and has a studio in Mumbai where she teaches pole dancing. It is an art form that is both sensuous and requires strength and skill.

Yogasanas

The Apsara energy is the energy of the svadishtana or the sacral chakra in the lower belly. It is active in the expression of our sensuality or sexual desires.

Focus on the hip openers for your yogic practice. This part has been stuck or damaged for many women, especially women who lose interest in sex after childbirth and motherhood. Remove the stuckness in the sacral chakra by doing the goddess pose. This is one of my favourite asanas. Other wonderful asanas for the sacral chakra are malasan, the titli or butterfly pose, and upavishtakonasanas which stretch and release the energies you need.

Actions

Invoking the Apsara involves stepping out of the comfort zone. This will seem strange and even self-indulgent to many Mas or Rishikas, who are quite disconnected with the feminine sensual self. It will seem risky to Kanyas, a waste of time to Veeras and an unnecessary deviation to the Ranis. But if you decide that you need the Apsara energy in your life to complete you, it is important to take some conscious actions. Actions allow access to a power, undertaking them does not mean you will become an Apsara.

One action is making changes to the exterior, which in turn leads to a change on the inside. All women know the power of a good hairstyle or the right clothes. These alone may not be enough, but it is a safe place to start. The 'shringar rasa' is one of the nine rasas in Indian classical art, whether it be dance, poetry, music or drama, and evokes beauty, attraction and romantic love.

The 'solah shringar' a bride does are sixteen different kinds of ornamentation. Adorning the self with ornaments is not just about enhancing physical beauty but also a way of acknowledging love for the self. So choose a style or a garment that is different from the usual and take some time over makeup. The sari for me is the garment that makes me feel most sensuous, yet I wear it only for special traditional occasions. I have long felt that it is impractical and less manageable than other clothes. However, when I decided to embrace my Apsara, I started wearing the sari more often, with matching accessories and a nose ring.

Another action to access the Apsara is to find a way of artistic self-expression. Start or reclaim an interest in painting, music, writing, dance or some other means of artistic self-expression. This is not a business venture or a routine practice but more of an indulgence, something you can treat yourself to.

Sometimes, the Apsara energy is needed in relationships that have become stale and dry or to initiate a new romantic relationship. Traditionally, women are not supposed to make the first move or even express interest in sex. The story of Shoorpanakha still has a firm hold on our imagination. This is changing to some extent but the cultural coding is strong.

Women who want more sizzle and sparkle in their lives will need to make the first move or reciprocate appropriately to an expression of interest from a potential partner. Many women's magazines and the internet are full of tips and techniques to rekindle the romantic flame. The dating app Bumble had over four million women users in India as of July 2020. The app allows women to make the first move and initiate contact with a potential partner. The Apsara power gives women the confidence to express their interest and take a step towards initiating a romantic relationship.

PARVEEN'S STORY

Parveen, a senior bank executive in her later forties, was a staunch Rishika. She was very proper, wore sober colours, had neatly cropped hair and a brisk no-nonsense way about her.

She saw no reason to change her appearance, she felt that it would damage her carefully built brand image. However, she felt something was missing in her life. She spoke about her teenage years as the 'best years of my life'.

She wrote poetry, which she neither showed to anyone nor published, but felt a deep sense of satisfaction when she wrote. She wrote in Urdu, which she felt was a sensuous language and ideal for poetry. This is the part she wanted to reclaim as a way of invoking her Apsara. Poetry allowed her free expression, which was lacking in other areas of her life. When she joined an online poetry group, she felt an immediate connection with other poets. Writing poetry was her way of accessing the Apsara.

Affirmations

These affirmations can be practiced by the Apsara who wants to grow in her power without energy drain, and also by those who want to invoke their Apsara power.

I attended a fabulous week-long women leadership programme at Esalen in California in the summer of 2019. At the end of it, we were asked to choose a name for ourselves which would symbolize the power we wanted to grow into. Mine was Wildcat Goddess. I did the unthinkable action of prowling around the room on my fours like a feline creature. It was a curiously liberating moment. I no longer crawl like a cat but I connect to that affirmation even now. You can always pick an affirmation that suits you the best. Here are some.

I am beautiful.
I have a beautiful gorgeous body.
I love my body.

I am sexy.
I am a free spirit.
I am a free-flowing river.
I am a wild woman.
I express myself freely and fully.
I am the Apsara in all her glory.
I am a celestial goddess dancing to a heavenly tune.

Practices to Gain Veera Power

The Veera power is resolute and action-oriented. It involves taking risks, being courageous in the face of challenges and taking tough decisions. It is easy to identify the need for this power, but not as easy to invoke it. For a typical Ma or Kanya, it is scary to take actions that require the Veera power. Ranis and Apsaras can adapt more easily to the Veera energy, if they sense that it can give them something that they need. Many Rishikas can intellectually rationalize and explain the absence of the Veera power, while secretly longing for that energy.

Body Practices

The body of a Veera is strong, tough and resolute. The energy flows outwards towards a goal and desired result. There are many ways to build the body of a Veera. The Veera does not have to be big and strong but has a presence that radiates energy and action orientation. A body practice that involves, strength, speed and results is the best way to connect to your Veera.

To start with, slightly increase the pace of your normal walk. Walk as though you need to get somewhere soon. Keep your back straight and look ahead as though you are seeing your destination. This is the Veera walk.

Strength training and rigorous exercise with fitness goals is another great way to build the Veera energy. I started working out with an instructor using weights and doing circuit training to build more strength in my body. Martial arts practices like karate, judo or kick-boxing are good Veera sports. Natural Veeras are often great athletes or have been involved in some competitive sport.

Running with a goal in mind is also a Veera pursuit. Others may run just for fun or for exercise, but the Veera trains for a marathon. If you are already a runner, then setting a goal and working towards it will invoke the Veera energy. If you enjoy swimming, then set a goal for the number of laps you will do in the pool. Other sports like tennis, badminton, and squash are also great for a Veera. These involve not just fast-paced physical activity, but tangible results for every match.

Yogasanas

The Veera power is focused on the manipura or the solar plexus chakra. The tight core and the fire in the belly comes from focus on this chakra. It is associated with confidence, self-esteem, purpose orientation and vitality. It gives the energy to get going and get things done. Many Mas who are exhausted by years of abnegation, Kanyas who have become passive and docile, and Rishikas who spend too much time over-thinking can all benefit from activating the manipura chakra.

Activate this chakra by doing asanas that strengthen the core. Boat pose or navasan, the bow pose or dhanurasan, all plank poses and asanas that ground you in strength are ideal. I personally like the veerabhadrasan, the warrior pose that gives both a resolute direction and stability. This is not the reckless warrior but one who goes into battle fully-armed and feet firmly on the ground. Another way to activate the vocal warrior is to work on the vishuddhi chakra or the throat chakra that gives you the power to speak the truth with courage. Veeras can also benefit from the vishuddhi, as they need to learn to speak the truth with tact and respect. Activate the throat chakra with a shoulder stand or sarvangasana, and the fish pose of matsyasana.

Actions

Most of us do set goals and work towards them. The energy and drive we have towards these goals can be different. Veeras thrive on goals and results. They feel lost if they don't see a tangible outcome for anything they do. A simple Veera action is making a list of things to do—every day.

This is a critical action for an Apsara or a Ma to take, because the Apsara loses track and becomes disorganized, while the Ma may let others dictate her day. Taking on a specific Veera project with milestones and non-negotiable deadlines is also important. Choose a couple of goals that involve a challenge and need you to stretch a bit. This will be a test of your Veera power.

Performing an act of courage and taking a risk acts as a great energy booster. Do something that scares you. Any act that involves overcoming your fears takes you closer to your Veera self. You don't have to do one big audacious thing. A series of small wins is also helpful. Veeras also have many fears but they keep pushing their boundaries. This, in turn, gives them the courage to take further risks.

I am a poor swimmer and am scared of being in any water body that is more than five-feet deep. It took me many years to learn swimming and my stamina in the water is poor. Yet I did not want to give up the opportunity to go snorkelling in the Great Barrier Reef during a holiday in Australia. After some hesitation, I took the plunge. Though I wore a life-jacket, it was scary to step into the ocean with my snorkelling mask. The experience was mind-blowing. I felt as though I was in a magical world. Later, I was also quite proud of myself for overcoming my fear. When I feel apprehensive about something, just recalling this experience gives me courage. Last year, I went parasailing for the very first time. The fact that I had done snorkelling earlier helped me to get over my fears and get up in the air.

Sometimes, you can prepare well for a challenge, sometimes you have to just do it. This is what the Veera is about.

SUSAN'S STORY

Susan was a junior lawyer in a law firm. She had moved to Mumbai after graduating from a prestigious law school. She was originally from Cochin and had led a sheltered life. Her boss, a respected senior lawyer, started making passes at her. He made her stay back late in office and ordered dinner for the two of them in his cabin. He would pass personal comments on her clothes and looks. He would rub against her when he came over to check her work. Susan had never experienced anything like this. She felt that she could not talk to anyone about this. The firm did not have a human resource person nor a complaints committee. She even thought of quitting the firm in disgust and fear.

Susan had been a cherished Kanya all her life. She had been brought up as a good girl and was aghast that she should be in such a situation. She felt ashamed and even blamed herself for somehow having attracted her boss' behaviour to herself.

Finally when Susan had made up her mind to quit, she confided in a friend. Her friend introduced her to an activist who worked with women who had been sexually harassed at the workplace. Susan needed to harness her Veera energy to tell her boss off without fear. Her activist told her about all options and Susan studied the relevant laws. She also rehearsed the lines she would say to her boss about his behaviour. She mustered courage and told her boss about her concerns and what action she planned to take. He realized she could not be taken for granted. Susan then asked to be assigned to another lawyer immediately.

She was glad that she did not quit the firm. This experience gave her a sense of power and she became more confident and forthright. She felt vindicated since she could stay on despite giving the feedback to her boss and telling him about the impact of his actions.

Affirmations

The Veera energy is about courage and achievement. The Veera energy power needs to be invoked when you need to banish your fears and move relentlessly towards a specific goal. The Veera is resilient and determined in the face of adversity.

The affirmations for a Veera will depend upon the specific context. Here are some common ones.

I am a winner.
I am brave and courageous.
I will overcome.
I am strong and powerful.

I will achieve my goals.
I am confident and capable.
I am determined.
I can make my own decisions.
I am totally badass!

Practices to Gain Rani Power

The Rani power is the ability to stay calm and composed during a crisis, weather storms with equanimity and maintain stability. The Rani is great at planning, organizing and being structured. She has a graceful unruffled air about her. Her presence is sedate and serene.

Body Practices

The Rani walks like a stately ship. Her steps are always measured, her pace steady and uniform. She does not seem to be in a hurry but quite sure of herself and where she needs to go. I know one of my neighbours is a Rani just by observing her walk. She walks the same circuit in exactly the same way, not stopping for anyone, not allowing anything else to break her rhythm.

The Rani likes a structured steady practice for her body as well. To invoke the Rani, choose a practice that consists of the same routines performed in a particular order. Do the surya namaskar, if you like yoga. Circuit training with repetitions also works. The movements should be precise, well-defined and harmonious. Ranis who swim are quite happy to go to the pool and do the same number of laps every day. Follow a pattern. Do not deviate from it. Stick to it even if you get bored quickly. Bring order and structure to your body routine.

You can choose a body practice that is about balancing and staying firm. Doing gymnastics, like walking on the balancing beam, is a good Rani practice. Walk with a book on your head or do a gentle version of the egg-and-spoon race. This will require focus and balance, which are Rani qualities.

Yogasanas

The mooladhara chakra or root chakra provides a stable foundation. It is the centre of balance and stability that grounds us to the basics. Focus on balancing poses like the tree pose or vrikshasana, trikonasana or triangle pose, tadasana or mountain pose, and ardachandrasana or half-moon pose. As you do these asanas, root yourself to the ground and feel your power to stay calm and rooted through turbulent times.

Actions

The Rani needs to take actions that will give her a sense of order, peace and calmness. An activity that is repetitive and involves being mindful in the present helps to invoke the Rani energy. These can be taken by a Rani who is facing a power block due to increased anxiety and stress. While she can thrive in troubled times, if things go beyond what she sees as her circle of control, she starts to panic.

For others who need the Rani power in their lives, practices that ground and bring stability will be helpful. The Apsaras—who tend to be flighty, restless and distracted—can benefit from some Rani actions. The Ma, who is stretched by multitasking and taking care of others' needs, also needs the Rani energy to draw boundaries and reclaim her space. The Veera, who is constantly firefighting needs to slow down and bring some order and calm into her life. The Rani energy will also help the Kanya to find her own space and take charge. Many Kanyas need to grow into Ranis when they are given additional responsibilities that can seem overwhelming or challenging.

One of the first actions in all the cases is to make a plan. We all do some level of planning. Apsaras plan only if they have to, they think it is boring. Veeras rush in quickly without a plan, they believe in action. Kanyas don't have a rigorous plan, they feel things will work out. Mas look to others to plan for them, and Rishikas get caught up in analysis and research stage for too long before coming to a plan.

The Rani loves plans. She is always prepared. She also has a Plan B. Taking time out to plan and prepare before an important project or task invokes the Rani energy. The plan has to be solid, not a random, hasty or vague idea. Taking time out every day to plan the day well is a good practice to feel the Rani power.

Meditation and chanting are also useful practices to bring in the Rani energy. Another practice to channelize the Rani power is cleaning and organizing. Start by cleaning the closet and drawers. Marie Kondo, the Japanese decluttering expert must be a heroine for Ranis. Bringing some order into chaos and removing clutter is a great way to invoke the Rani energy. Organize things into categories, label them and enjoy the sight of nice orderly rows and columns. This activity has to be done as a practice, not as a dreaded chore. Bring an intention to the action and enjoy it to truly feel the Rani power.

The Rani energy has a strong connection to the earth. It is a grounded steady energy. Earthing is a practice that involves walking barefoot on grass or earth. While this practice is supposed to have therapeutic effects, it is also a way of grounding yourself psychologically. Standing firmly on the earth and drawing on the grounding energy also works. Sitting still with your feet flat on the ground is a simple steadying practice. Feeling the solid ground beneath your feet is a way to feel supported and stable.

ABHA'S STORY

I knew of Abha's story from a friend who is a part of the Soka Gakkai circle.

Abha was going through a tough time. She was a natural Rani and led a peaceful, well-ordered life. Suddenly she was hit by multiple adversities. Her mother was diagnosed with cancer. Her teenage son did not get the results he was expecting in his Class XII board exams, which impacted his career choices. Her husband's business partner cheated him out of a large sum of money. Abha felt her neat orderly world had come crashing down.

She started having panic attacks and could not sleep. Things worsened. Even her daughter, to whom she was close, started feeling neglected and helpless. A friend introduced Abha to the practice of chanting through a Buddhist Sokka Gakkai circle. Abha was not a religious woman but just the practice of chanting, repeating the same lines many times over, gave her strength and peace.

Abha also started going for morning walks for twenty minutes at the same time every day and would practice her affirmations at this time. Over a period of time, she was able to become more calm and resilient. When her mother passed away two years later, Abha was able to manage her grief and be a source of support for others. Her son took a gap year after college and found a course that opened up new possibilities for him.

Affirmations

The affirmations to invoke the Rani focus on her good qualities and her view of the world. The dominant Rani is prone to anxiety and worry, so her affirmations help to calm her down. For those who need the Rani energy, the affirmations bring confidence and a sense of control.

Here are some affirmations for the Rani power.

I am stable.
I can handle anything.
I am in control.
This too shall pass.
I am good at planning.
I am strong and resilient.
I am calm and composed.
I am peaceful.
I can manage well.
I am good at solving complex problems.

Practices to Gain Ma Power

The power of the Ma is the power of compassion and care. The Ma is empathetic, sensitive, generous and unselfish. The Ma also has a creative side to her that is nourishing, generative and life-affirming. The Ma is a champion of the underdog and feels deeply for the oppressed and dispossessed. She draws her power from listening to others and understanding their needs. These are critical qualities for a leader. Her heart is vast and open to others.

Body Practices

The Ma has an invitational and inclusive energy. Her pace is unhurried and she stops to connect with the world around her. Sometimes, she tends to stoop, as though she is carrying the burden of the world upon her. A Ma in her full power is a mother goddess—a warm, loving being who offers the shade of her presence to all those who pass by.

The Ma energy is closely connected to nature, mindful walking that involves being fully present to the world around you is a lovely way to connect to yourself. Ideally, walk in the park admiring the nature around you. Or go on a trek in the mountains. Look at the flowers, hear the birdsong, become alive to the glory of the trees.

Body practices to invoke the Ma involve opening the heart and mind to others and the world. A practice with open hand movements and a slow pace suit the Ma. A practice that involves others without being aggressively competitive works well. A group yoga class is one of the best options. Resolute Veeras will benefit from a slow yin yoga class or a tai chi class. An exercise form that involves stretching and opening of the joints works well to invoke the Ma energy.

Individual body practices are also effective. Put on some slow music and do free-flow dancing ensuring that the body is not strained or hurt in any way. Hold an intention to open and become flexible.

Yogasanas

The asanas to invoke the Ma activate the heart or anahata chakra. Do the asanas with the spirit of connection and empathy. The baby cobra pose, the camel pose or ushtrasana (sitting or standing), the bridge pose or sethubandasana, and the wheel pose chakrasana help to clear the heart chakra. Think about a situation where you want to be compassionate and giving as you do the poses and invite that energy into your life.

The Ma who has experienced a power block and has become a martyr, or one who smothers others, needs these asanas to reclaim her loving energy.

Actions

Those in need of the Ma energy need to take actions that involve connection to others. Care is an important aspect of the Ma energy. The Ma—who feels burnt out and exhausted because of working too much and too hard to please others—needs self-care practices to energize herself. The Ma often feels that self-care is selfish but she could have reached the point when she feels resentful of others and their actions are forced and inauthentic. So, if you are a dominant Ma who needs to reconnect to her power, take time out. Get a massage, indulge yourself in something you value. Get someone else to pamper you. You can't serve from an empty vessel. Nourish and fill yourself with what you need.

Veeras can benefit from the Ma energy too, if they have become too task-focused and driven. Their ambition makes them blind to other people's needs. Veeras believe that they are doing their best for others, but their actions will not always have a positive impact. Ranis benefit from the Ma energy when they become too stuck to rules and regimen, instead of seeing the impact of these rules on others. They fear chaos if people don't adhere to the rules and refuse to listen to alternate viewpoints. The Apsaras are drawn to a Ma, but often forget that the Ma has her needs too. Apsaras can become selfish and irresponsible in the pursuit of their dreams. They have a tendency to believe that others are as invested in their dreams and will naturally support the Apsara. The Rishika, meanwhile, is lost in her remote tower and does not even notice the people around her. The Kanya adapts easily to the Ma energy, if she feels that it will give her acceptance. But her acts are not consistent or grounded in authenticity. She can play the Ma role without embracing the power of the Ma.

Some consistent actions will help all the other five archetypes who need to invoke the Ma energy:

- Adopt the twenty-one day kindness challenge. This involves performing an act of kindness for twenty-one days consecutively. It could just paying someone a genuine compliment, giving a note of appreciation, or helping someone in need. Giving a donation by clicking a button is not counted. It has to involve other people.
- Engage in an activity that is grounding and nourishing. Cooking with love and feeding others is a typical Ma action. Everyone may cook, but the kind of cooking that a Ma does is not necessarily a creative act or an accomplishment. It is a simple act of nourishing others.
- Volunteering your time and effort is also a good way to invoke the Ma energy. This act needs to involve engaging and doing something for people. Teaching others, working with your hands to build and create something, serving food to others—all these activities done with the spirit of service will help to invoke the Ma energy.

One of the actions that helped me to invoke the Ma energy was to get trained as a coach. As a Rishika, I sometimes could not connect to others' needs easily. My approach was to tell and dazzle rather than listen and support. I believed that a logical explanation combined with articulate communication was the best way to influence and persuade people. Coaching taught me to listen patiently, become consciously empathetic and focus entirely on my clients' needs and goals. This is something, I can bring not just to my work but to all people interactions.

GUNEET'S STORY

Guneet, an entrepreneur who had grown her marketing agency to a twenty-five-person firm, was a dominant Rani and Veera. She led a disciplined, driven life. A sudden spate of attrition in her company made her re-think her approach and leadership style. Guneet felt the need to invoke her Ma energy and become more empathetic.

I worked with her as a coach to help her adapt her leadership style. An analogy and new mindset that helped her was to see her role as a gardener growing her people, not a ringmaster with a whip. To help her adapt, she also began gardening at her home. She started vegetable gardening in a small way with a few potted plants, growing cherry tomatoes, chillies and some herbs. The process of tending to plants and waiting for the fruit of her labour helped her to invoke the Ma energy. She learnt patience and the art of cultivation.

Affirmations

The Ma who fears becoming redundant or abandoned needs affirmations to connect to the positive side of her power. Many Mas become clingy, possessive and needy in their pursuit of being needed and valued. Others need to invoke the energy to form better connections, show empathy and generosity. These are some affirmations for the Ma:

I am generous and giving.
I am a warm, loving person.
I am needed and cherished.
I nourish life.
I am the nurturer.
I care about the well-being and welfare of others.
I value all the connections and relationships in my life.
I am the source of creation.
I am unselfish.
I am the mother goddess in her full power.

Practices to Gain Rishika Power

Rishikas get their power from knowledge, rational thinking, intellectual acumen and the connection to a larger purpose in their life. The Rishika's ability to detach herself from messy emotions is her strength and cutting through a situation with razor-sharp precision is her power. She has great clarity of thought and speech. She has high moral principles and the ability to pursue these. The Rishika can be a great teacher, mentor and guru.

Body Practices

The Rishika walks with a noble steady pace. She could appear to be lost in her own thoughts. Her mind could be cooking up several ideas and solving problems. A Rishika who is more mystical may seem to glide gracefully on the ground. She has a wise and serene presence.

The Rishika energy requires a practice that is rigorous but not physically intense. Her movements are graceful and sharp.

Rishika energy is also channelized by a combination of music and dance. The spiritual music of the Sufis and Bauls, which also involves movement of the body in a divine dance, allows for the Rishika energy to flow.

Aikido, the Japanese martial art developed by Morihei Ueshiba, is a wonderful practice to bring out the Rishika power. According to the founder's philosophy, the primary goal in the practice of aikido is to overcome oneself, instead of cultivating violence or aggressiveness (David, 2015). Ueshiba used the phrase 'masakatsu agatsu katsuhayabi' (true victory, final victory over oneself, here and now) to refer to this principle. I had a brief experience of this with Wendy Palmer at a Leadership Embodiment workshop a few years ago.

Body practices that are sensuous, competitive or just fun are to be avoided if you need to feel the Rishika energy.

Yogasanas

The crown chakra or saharara chakra is the doorway to higher consciousness and spiritual knowledge. It is the doorway to self-reflection, contemplation and self-realization. It helps invoke the Rishika energy. Combining the asanas of the ajna and sahasrara chakras can be very powerful to release the Rishika energy.

Do the headstand or shirshasan for the crown chakra, upavishtakonasan for the ajna chakra, and forward bends like the prasarita paddotasana to invoke both.

Actions

Some women naturally grow to the Rishika stage after several life experiences. They have learnt on the journey and have performed the actions to embrace the Rishika energy.

The width and breadth of experience gives them wisdom and clarity. Others will need to harness the Rishika energy depending upon their life situation and context.

Veeras who rush to make decisions and value quick action need the Rishika energy to weigh their decisions and take a call in the interest of everyone. Ranis need the Rishika energy to examine age-old traditions and customs that they may be following blindly. They need the Rishika power to spur them to new actions and adapt to change through knowledge and analysis.

The Apsaras use the Rishika energy to ground themselves. Apsaras who feel that they are not taken seriously need to invoke their Rishika power to bring gravitas to the situation. The Rishika power can help them to manage their mood swings and emotional upheavals. Kanyas, who can be naïve and blindly optimistic, require the Rishika power for clarity and correct decision-making. Acquiring the Rishika power will enable them to be taken seriously and grow in their chosen area. A Ma, who could be blind to the failings of her loved ones and keeps short-changing herself, needs the Rishika energy to find more confidence and assert her place in the world.

An action to harness the Rishika power is to learn a new skill and acquire knowledge. The process of learning and mastering something new takes you closer to your inner Rishika. In the movie *English Vinglish*, the heroine Shashi, a typical Ma, enrols in an English class and grows through this process. It gives her new knowledge, confidence and the respect of her family. The learning cannot be a forced learning for survival, it needs to be embraced with curiosity and openness. This learning is different from just learning in a classroom to pass exams. This is voluntary learning, it could be just for the sake of knowing something new or with some higher goal in mind.

Reading is a way to invoke the Rishika energy. Reading fiction opens our minds to new worlds and new people. Reading non-fiction gives us access to new knowledge, research and a new way of looking at the world.

Meditation is a good Rishika practice. Many Rishikas enjoy the act of meditation, sitting still and enjoying the silence. Other forms of meditation include losing yourself in an activity that puts you in a state of immersive engagement in an art or even cooking, being mindful to every nuanced act, is a Rishika power. Mindfulness is the quality needed in any action to invoke the Rishika energy.

Spiritual practice is also a way of connecting with the Rishika power. Not all Rishikas are spiritual or religious. However, the process of enquiry and reflection that a spiritual practice involves is what draws the Rishika. Unlike the Rani who derives satisfaction from following traditions and customs as a way of maintaining a norm, the Rishika is drawn to religious discourse. She likes to question and even debate the nature of being, the existence of god and delve deeper into religious texts to understand the truth. She may be drawn to a guru, but she will not accept the guru's teaching or philosophy blindly.

KAMAL'S STORY

Kamal was a young associate in a large consulting organization and one of my first coaching clients. She was referred for coaching after her performance review, having received feedback that she was not assertive during client interactions and meetings with senior partners. Kamal was a Kanya who dressed casually, giggled a lot and chattered non-stop. She was surprised that she had been hired by the consulting firm – she did not think she was 'that type'. She ruefully admitted that she was not taken seriously by others and given opportunities to speak at meetings. The senior men were 'very nice' but did not ask for her inputs. Kamal felt that this behaviour on their part was natural and did not feel that it could be changed. 'I am so junior. How can I speak in front of seniors who have so much knowledge and experience?' she asked. Kamal needed to invoke the Rishika power and develop a presence with more gravitas if she wanted to succeed in her career. She started preparing for the meetings and researched more about the industry and company that she was working with. She listened carefully to others' inputs and took notes which she referred to in her conversation. She structured her conversation and modified her tone of voice when she spoke. She recorded herself speaking and, along with my feedback, became aware of the changes she needed to make in her presence and presentation. She started taking herself seriously, leading others to take her seriously as well.

Affirmations

The Rishika who feels that she has lost her power needs affirmations to reconnect to it. Rishikas are prone to self-doubt and anxiety when they are confronted by insoluble problems or when they face situations which make them feel emotionally vulnerable. These are times to invoke their power and connect to strengths they already possess. Those who need the *Rishika* power will also benefit from these affirmations.

I am smart and intelligent.
I am knowledgeable.
I am an expert in my field.
I bring clarity to confusion.
I bring a depth of insight.
I am wise and wonderful.
I am aligned to my purpose.
I hold my wisdom with lightness.
I embody grace and gravitas.
I see through artifice and speak the truth.

Epilogue

Powerful is not a self-help book with a handy list of 'to-dos' nor is it just an assessment that slots you in a particular category. I have used many psychometric instruments in the course of my work. I don't believe any single framework can capture the beauty and complexity of human beings. The six powers are guides. They can be weapons. They are as good as the user. They need to be understood and applied mindfully. The powers are not cast in stone. No one is ever just one archetype. We evolve, we change and yet we do remain true to our essence. We adapt to contexts. We revert to our core powers once we are back in our comfort zone.

Writing *Powerful* has been a transformational journey for me. The idea had been swirling in my head for a few years, but it took me some time to heed the call. I faced the demons of self-doubt and fear, 'What if this is all nonsense? You will be seen as a man-hater.' 'Women don't really need you to empower them.' 'You don't have a Ph.d.'

I had to use my own Veera energy to forge through. I had to call upon my Rani power to be disciplined to the craft and get down to the act of writing instead of tossing ideas in my head. I overcame my innate Rishika power block and shared the concept with several women. Every woman I spoke to could immediately connect to the archetypes. As I talked with my friends, they started using the terms: 'I need to awaken my Apsara.' 'My Rani and Rishika are always fighting with each other.'

This works.

I would love to see women across the world, and especially in India, use the knowledge of the powers as a doorway to conversations with others—men and women. This knowledge can be a catalyst for growth and wholeness. This knowledge can help to navigate the typical challenges that women face: dealing with gender discrimination, sexual harassment at work, negotiating for ourselves, balancing home and work. Some are universal issues and some are specific to an individual. The knowledge of our power patterns can help us make informed choices about life partners and life-changing events.

This book can be a guide to choose a line of work in line with one's core strengths while being open to learning new behaviours. As we lay claim to power in the outside world, we also need to claim the power within us. I hope this book brings alive that power which is there not just in some of us, but in all of us, all the time.

This book is a part of the Powerfulife system that I have created to enable women to lead powerful lives. Please visit the website www.powerfulife.in. You can take an assessment to get your power profile and identify your dominant and shadow powers. There are a variety of resources available to tap into your inner power and sustain the changes you want to make in your life.

The Powers at a Glance

Theme	Kanya: The Good girl	Apsara: The Seductive Beauty	Veera: The Rebel Warrior	Rani: The Noble Queen	Ma: The Nurturing Caregiver	Rishika: The Wise Woman
Qualities	Optimistic, trusting, innocent, playful, sweet	Charming, sensual, alluring, wild, passionate	Aggressive, bold, breaks rules, fighter, gritty, tenacious	Stable, steady, predictable, calm, composed, organized	Giver, caring, sacrificing own needs, earthy, fecund, nourishing, helpful	Seeker, explorer, wise, curious, knowledgeable, learner, mystical
Core needs	Acceptance, nurturing from a parent	Self-expression, freedom	Self-determination, achievement	Order, stability, harmony	To be needed, to belong	Mastery and contribution

To get a better understanding of your powers, take the Powerfulife Assessment at www.powerfulife.in and get your own Power Profile.

Theme	Kanya: The Good girl	Apsara: The Seductive Beauty	Veera: The Rebel Warrior	Rani: The Noble Queen	Ma: The Nurturing Caregiver	Rishika: The Wise Woman
Limiting belief	I have to be good to get acceptance.	I will be loved only if I am attractive. I have to pay a price for my freedom.	Life is a battle and I have to fight.	I am the responsible one who has to hold it together. Change is dangerous.	Others are more important than me. I am valued only for what I do for others.	I get respect by negating my femininity. I don't need other people.
Power blocks	Weak, submissive, gullible, childish	Promiscuous, irresponsible, wanton, wild, melancholic, self-destructive	Dominating, vengeful, reckless, destructive	Rigid, stubborn, fearful	Smothering, over-protective, martyr	Aloof, distant, a pedantic, unrealistic, arrogant

To get a better understanding of your powers, take the Powerfulife Assessment at www.powerfulife.in and get your own Power Profile.

Theme	Kanya: The Good girl	Apsara: The Seductive Beauty	Veera: The Rebel Warrior	Rani: The Noble Queen	Ma: The Nurturing Caregiver	Rishika: The Wise Woman
Emotional drain	Shame	Melancholy	Rage	Anxiety	Guilt	Frigidity
Cultural context	Obedience is a virtue. Innocence is rewarded. Loss of innocence or virginity is punished.	Sexual power of women is dangerous. Attractive women cannot be taken seriously.	Women don't fight in wars. Women don't have the right to self-determination.	Women can rule with the consent of men. Women should be content to rule over the kitchen.	Mother sacrifices for others. Only mothers of sons are valued. Motherhood is the ultimate destiny of a woman.	Women can become wise only when they become old. Being knowledgeable and well read is not a feminine quality.

To get a better understanding of your powers, take the Powerfulife Assessment at www.powerfulife.in and get your own Power Profile.

Theme	Kanya: The Good girl	Apsara: The Seductive Beauty	Veera: The Rebel Warrior	Rani: The Noble Queen	Ma: The Nurturing Caregiver	Rishika: The Wise Woman
Relationship with men	Needs approval and protection of men	Needs to attract men	Identifies as man	Aligns with men	Takes care of men	Indifferent to men
Career choices	Hospitality, sales, public relations, customer service	Model, actor, artist, dancer, tour guide, hospitality	Activist, entrepreneur, lawyer, business management	Office work, project management, finance, operations	Nurse, service, home-based chef, child-care	Teacher, healer, counsellor, research consultant
Practices to gain the power	Bollywood dancing, playing with children, amusement park rides	Dressing up, wearing bright colours, makeup, jewellery, belly dancing	Krav maga, karate, strength training, boxing, running	Yoga, circuit training, making lists, housekeeping, work, classical dance	Volunteer work, cooking, baking, baby sitting, adopting a pet	Yoga, meditation tai chi, reading

To get a better understanding of your powers, take the Powerfulife Assessment at www.powerfulife.in and get your own Power Profile.

Bibliography

2: Women and Power

Amnesty International. www.amnestyusa.org. 23 January 2020.

Beard, Mary, *Women and Power: A Manifesto*, London: Profile Books, 2017.

Harari, Yuval Noah, *Sapiens: A Brief History of Humankind*, translated by Yuval Noah Harari with John Purcell and Haim Watzman, London: Harvill Secker, 2014.

Hinchliffe, Emma, 'The number of female CEOs in the Fortune 500 hits an all-time record', *Fortune*, 18 May 2020, https://fortune.com/2020/05/18/women-ceos-fortune-500-2020/

'India: Where a woman is killed every hour for dowry', *IndiaSpend*, 17 September 2013. https://www.indiaspend.com/india-where-a-woman-is-killed-every-hour-for-dowry-68340/

Indo-Asian News Service (IANS), 'Man kills daughter for talking to boyfriend late at night', *New Indian Express*, 18 November 2019. https://www.newindianexpress.com/nation/2019/nov/18/up-honour-killing-man-kills-daughter-for-talking-to-boyfriend-late-at-night-2063401.html

Inter-Parliamentary Union, 'Global data on national parliaments', last modified on 1 October 2020, https://data.ipu.org/women-averages?month=10&year=2020&op=Show+averages&form_build_id=form-j2oESLcRgyixgqo9OQ7slMHQHKmRNOE_1dOEsd-e894&form_id=ipu__women_averages_filter_form

Kalidasa, *Shakuntala*, translated by Arthur W. Ryder, Cambridge,ON: Sanksrit Series, In Parentheses Publications, 1999. (The original work, *Abhigyana Shakuntalam*, is dated to between 1 BCE–4 CE).

Keltner, Dacher, *The Power Paradox: How We Gain and Lose Influence*, New York: Penguin Press, 2016.

King, Martin Luther, 'Where do we go from here?', (n.a.). https://kinginstitute.stanford.edu/king-papers/documents/where-do-we-go-here-address-delivered-eleventh-annual-sclc-convention

O'Neill, Aaron, 1 March 2021 'Number of countries where the highest position of executive power was held by a woman, in each year from 1960–2021', *Statista*, accessed on 20 January 2021. https://www.statista.com/statistics/1058345/countries-with-women-highest-position-executive-power-since-1960/

Rajalakshmi, T.K., 'Sati and the verdict', *Frontline*, 12 March 2004. http://www.hinduonnet.com/fline/fl2105/stories/20040312002504600.htm

'Rape is consensual: Inside Haryana's rape culture', *The Quint*, 7 April 2018. https://www.thequint.com/videos/documentaries/rape-is-consensual-inside-haryanas-rape-culture

Roy, Pulaha, 'India saw almost 1,500 acid attacks in five years', *India Today*, 12 January 2020. https://www.indiatoday.in/diu/story/india-saw-almost-1-500-acid-attacks-in-five-years-1636109-2020-01-12#:~:text=And%20India%20Today%20Data%20Intelligence,at%20309%2C%20with%20319%20victims

Salyer, Kirsten, and Oliver Cann, 'Everything you need to know about the gender gap in 2020', *World Economic Forum*, last modified 17 Dec 2019. https://www.weforum.org/agenda/2019/12/gender-gap-report-gender-parity-how-to-speed-up-progress/

Sharma, Kavita, 'Mahabharata Through the Eyes of Women', in, *Women's Studies in India: Contours of Change*, Malashri Lal and Sukrita Pal Kumar (Eds), Shimla: Indian Institute of Advanced Study, 2002.

Shukla, Pankhuri, Shubam Mishra's YouTube Is India's Rape culture in a nutshell', 13 July 2020. www.thequint.com

Tagore, Rabindranath, *Chokher Bali*, translated by Radha Chakravarty, Gurugram: Penguin Random House, 2012.

Troll Patrol India: Exposing Online Abuse Faced by Women Politicians in India, *Amnesty Decoders*, https://decoders.amnesty.org/projects/troll-patrol-india

World Bank, 29 January 2021 'Labor force participation rate, female (% of female population ages 15+) (modeled ILO estimate) – India', *The World Bank*, accessed on 10 October 2020. https://data.worldbank.org/indicator/SL.TLF.CACT.FE.ZS?locations=IN

3: The Six Sources of Power

Bolen, Jean Shinoda, *Goddesses in Everywoman: Powerful Archetypes in Women's Lives*, New York, NY: Quill, an imprint of HarperCollins Publishers, 2004.

'Boost for "Beti Bachao Beti Padhao" campaign: Haryana now on path to recovery', FE Online, 13 January 2020. https://www.financialexpress.com/lifestyle/health/boost-for-beti-bachao-beti-padhao-campaign-haryana-now-on-path-to-recovery/1821035/

Divakaruni, Chitra Banerjee, *The Palace of Illusions*, New Delhi: Picador, 2008.

Divakaruni, Chitra Banerjee, *The Forest of Enchantments*, Noida: HarperCollins India, 2019.

Eldredge, John, *The Way of the Wild Heart: A Map for the Masculine Journey*, Nashville, TN: Nelson Books, 2006.

Harris, Massimilla, and Bud Harris, *Into the Heart of the Feminine: Facing the Death Mother Archetype to Reclaim Love, Strength, and Vitality*, Ashville, NC: Daphne Publications, 2015.

Jung, Carl Gustav, *The Archetypes and the Collective Unconscious*, second edition, Abingdon: Routledge, 1991.

Kokkoka, Pandit, *The Hindu Secrets of Love: Rati Rahasya of Kokkoka*, Mumbai: D.B. Taraporevela & Sons, 1965.

Moore, Robert and Douglas Gillette, *King, Warrior, Magician, Lover: Rediscovering the Archetypes of the Mature Masculine*, San Francisco, CA: HarperSanFrancisco, 1992.

Shenoy, Preeti, *The Rule Breakers*, Chennai: Westland Publications, 2018

Subramanian, Nirupama, *Keep the Change*, Noida: HarperCollins India, 2010.

Subramanian, Nirupama, *Intermission*, Noida: HarperCollins India, 2012.

Tripathi, Amish, *Sita: Warrior of Mithila*, Chennai: Westland Publications, 2017.

4: Kanya: The Good Girl

'Boost for "Beti Bachao Beti Padhao" campaign: Haryana now on path to recovery', *FE Online*, 13 January 2020. https://www.financialexpress.com/lifestyle/health/boost-for-beti-bachao-beti-padhao-campaign-haryana-now-on-path-to-recovery/1821035/

'Sex Survey 2019: Virginity important for 53%, majority against filming sex,' https://www.indiatoday.in/lifestyle/story/the-more-things-change-1614722-2019-11-01

5: Apsara: The Seductive Beauty

Archer, W.G., *India and Modern Art*, New York, NY: The Macmillan Co., 1959.

Chughtai, Ismat, *The Quilt: Stories*, translated by M. Asaduddin, New Delhi: Penguin Evergreens, Penguin Books India, 2011.

Dalmia, Yashodhara, *Amrita Sher-Gil: A Life*, New Delhi, Penguin Viking, 2006.

Dutt, Nirupama, When Amrita Sher-Gil vowed to seduce Khushwant Singh to take revenge on his wife, Scroll.in, 30 January 2017. https://scroll.in/magazine/827982/when-amrita-sher-gil-vowedto-seduce-khushwant-singh-to-take-revenge-on-his-wife

Gilbert, Elizabeth, *Eat, Pray, Love: One Woman's Search for Everything*, London: Bloomsbury, 2007.

Singh, Nandita, 'Remembering Amrita Sher-Gil, one who loved sex, art and India, and never said sorry for it', *The Print*, 5 December. https://theprint.in/features/remembering-amrita-sher-gil-one-who-loved-sex-art-and-india-and-never-said-sorry-for-it/158839/

Tharu, Susie and K. Lalitha, *Women Writing in India: 600 B.C. to Present, Volume* 1, New Delhi: Oxford University Press, 1992.

Wieckowski, Ania G. 'For women in business, beauty is a liability', *Harvard Business Review*, November-December 2019. https://hbr.org/2019/11/for-women-in-business-beauty-is-a-liability

6. Veera: The Rebel Warrior

Mitra, Dola, *Decoding Didi: Making Sense of Mamata Banerjee*, India: Rupa Publications, 2014

Paul, Shutapa, *Didi: The Untold Mamata Banerjee*, India: Penguin, 2018.

7. Rani: The Noble Queen

Annapoorna, Indra Nooyi: *A Biography*, Rajpal and Sons, 2015.

Austen, Jane, *Sense and Sensibility*, n.a., 1811. (Published anonymously in three volumes in 1811)

Baillee, Joanna, 'Ahalya Baee', n.a., 1849. (Printed for private circulation)

Burnison, Gary, 'How Pepsi's Indra Nooyi learned to be a CEO', Fast Company, last accessed 13 April 2021. https://www.fastcompany.com/1750645/how-pepsis-indra-nooyi-learned-be-ceo

Hindustan Times, https://www.hindustantimes.com/bollywood/ madhuri-dixit-savoured-being-a-housewife-in-the-us-used-to-cook-at-dawn-for-husband-dr-shriram-nene/story- AHkHgLoYHJb5iVnT8Ks1pL.html

Organisation for Economic Co-operation and Development, 'Employment: Time spent in paid and unpaid work, by sex', *OECD.Stat*, last modified 05 February 2021. https://stats.oecd.org/index.aspx?queryid=54757

Nooyi's biodata on Linkedin: https://www.linkedin.com/ public-profile/in/indranooyi?challengeId=AQEXGfG1RaHCjwAAAXd3dRQ 64wT58tqCsbi4dw99pmBt6sFyMngdZ2IYwBKeQ5reAbB_kcTzcPDXAhCaK6Qq6rXbj6sP6_TDhw&submissionId=d8917b2a-862a-6116-469a-d2b100d81373

Reingold, Jennifer, 'PepsiCo's CEO was right. Now what?', Fortune, last accessed 13 April 2021. https://fortune.com/2015/06/05/pepsico-ceo-indra-nooyi/

Seth, Vikram, *A Suitable Boy*, New Delhi: Penguin India, 1993.

Startup Stories, https://www.startupstories.in/topten/motivational-quotes-from-indra-nooyi-the-ex-ceo-of-pepsico

8. Ma: The Nurturing Caregiver

Castro, Joseph, 'How a mother's love changes a child's brain', *LiveScience*, 30, January 2012. https://www.livescience.com/18196-maternal-support-child-brain.html

Lewis, C.S., *The Complete Chronicles of Narnia*, New York, NY: HarperFestival, 2010. (First published as seven books in the 1950s)

Myss, Caroline, 'Appendix: A gallery of archetypes', myss.com, n.d., https://www.myss.com/free-resources/sacred-contracts-and-your-archetypes/appendix-a-gallery-of-archtypes/

Neumann, Eric, *The Great Mother: An Analysis of the Archetype*, translated by Ralph Manheim, Princeton, NJ: Princeton University Press, 1991. (First published in 1955)

TheNewsMinute, 'Coimbatore AIADMK workers build temple for former CM J Jayalalithaa', 19 July 2019, https://www.thenewsminute.com/article/coimbatore-aiadmk-workers-build-temple-former-cm-j-jayalalithaa-105744

Vivekananda, Swami, 'Women of India', a lecture delivered at the Shakespeare Club House, in Pasadena, California, 18 January 1900. https://www.ramakrishnavivekananda.info/vivekananda/volume_8/lectures_and_discourses/women_of_india.htm

9. Rishika: The Wise Woman

Aravamudan, Krishnan, *Pure Gems of Ramayanam*, Noida: Partridge India, 2014.

Jebaraj, Priscilla, 'Romila Thapar declines to send her CV to JNU', updated 6 September 2019. https://www.thehindu.com/news/national/romila-thapar-declines-to-send-her-cv-to-jnu/article29344139.ece

Mukhoty, Ira, *Heroines: Powerful Indian Women of Myth and History*, New Delhi: Aleph Books, 2017.

Partners for Law in Development, *Targeting of Women as Witches-Trends, Practices and Law in Northern, Western, Eastern and North Eastern Regions of India*, 2012. http:// pldindia.org/wp-content/uploads/2013/02/WH-Report-. pdf

Srivastava, Amitabh, 'Over 2000 women killed in India for practising "black magic" in 14 years', 20 June 2016, last accessed on 13 April 2021. https://www.indiatoday.in/india/story/over-2000- women-killed-in-india-for-practicing-black-magic-in-14- years-15280-2016-06-20

Steinhauer, Jason. 'Who writes history? Romila Thapar and the textbooks of India', 31 March 2015. https://blogs.loc.gov/kluge/2015/03/who-writes-history/

10: The Journey to Becoming Powerful

Williamson, Marianne, *A Return to Love: Reflections on the Principles of 'A Course in Miracles'*, New York, NY: HarperCollins, 1992.

11: Practices to Invoke Your Power

Byrne, Rhonda, *The Secret*, Cammeray, NSW: Atria Books, 2006.

Hay, Louise L., *You Can Heal Your Life*, Carlsbad, CA: Hay House Inc., 1999.

Jones, David, *Martial Arts Training in Japan: A Guide for Westerners*. Clarendon, VT: Tuttle Publishing, 2015.

Acknowledgements

A version of this book had been in my mind for a long time. I am grateful to all the people who helped me on the journey to grow an idea from inception to completion.

My introduction to the world of personal transformation began in 2010 when I was selected to be a part of the external facilitator group at Mckinsey & Co. I learnt about archetypes, limiting beliefs and the different pathways to grow into our full potential. My colleagues in the community, now known as Aberkyn, have been amazing co-travellers and each one has in some way been a part of my transformational journey. A special thanks to the Apsaras—Leela Kirloskar, Savitri Rao and Rhea D'souza—for the insights and validation generously shared during a sunny afternoon in Lisbon.

My business partner at GLOW—Growing Leadership of Women—Aparna Mathur, has been a great sounding board and support for all ideas. We look forward to more enriching work with women.

I am grateful to psychometrician and Jungian psychologist Vijai Pandey for his feedback and perspective on the model, and the partnership to create a unique assessment tool that will bring *Powerful* to life.

Thank you to Ahana Sehgal who helped me with the bibliography and some of the research.

A big thank you to the team at HarperCollins, especially my editor Prema Govindan for championing this book and believing in the Six Powers.

Thank you to the amazing powerful people who endorsed the book even before the release—Kiran Mazumdar-Shaw, Debjani Ghosh, Shital Kakkar Mehra, Chitra Banerjee Divakaruni, Kaveree Bamzai and Shiv Shivakumar.

My family has been a constant source of support and motivation through the writing of the book.

My mother, who always believed that I would write another book.

My sister Niranjana, writing consultant, for reading the manuscript and giving her inputs.

Rajesh, my husband, who gives me the space to start writing and never fails to give me the nudge to complete it. Kaavya, my daughter, for being the amazing young woman who constantly inspires me with her clarity, kindness, intelligence and awesomeness.

I also drew inspiration and insights from all the women I have coached and trained, who shared their stories of struggle and success. I drew confidence from my women friends who received the ideas in *Powerful* with great enthusiasm and connected it to their lives. This book would not have been possible without them.

About the Author

Nirupama Subramanian is the co-founder of GLOW, Growing Leadership of Women, an organization that enables gender equality and inclusion. She is an ICF-trained Professional Certified Coach (P.C.C.) and a leadership-development facilitator with over twenty-five years of experience. She has trained and coached over 20,000 people across seventy-five organizations. Nirupama is also the co-founder of My Daughter Is Precious, a non-profit that provides funding and mentoring for young women to complete their undergraduate education. Nirupama is the author of the best-selling novels *Keep the Change* and *Intermission*. She has written for a variety of publications, including the *Times of India*, *Hindustan Times* and *National Geographic Traveller*, among others, and has won several awards for her writing. To know more, visit www.nirupamasubramanian.com and www.powerfulife.in.